This paper was originally presented at the Chinese Council for
Advanced Policy Studies–RAND Corporation–National Defense
University 26th Annual Conference on the People's Liberation Army
on November 21–22, 2014, at the RAND Corporation office in
Arlington, Virginia. The conference series is co-sponsored by the
Chinese Council for Advanced Policy Studies in Taiwan, the RAND
Corporation, and the Center for the Study of Chinese Military
Affairs, Institute for National Strategic Studies, at the National
Defense University (NDU).

Because of the length of the analysis, the conference organizers
agreed to publish this paper as part of the China Strategic
Perspectives series from NDU Press in order to make all data
available. Other papers from the conference are currently in revision
for future publication in an edited volume.

Cover photo: Chairman of the Joint Chiefs of Staff Admiral Mike Mullen
visits Chinese People's Liberation Army Navy submarine *Yuan* at Zhoushan
Naval Base in China, July 13, 2011 (DOD/Chad J. McNeeley)

Chinese Military Diplomacy, 2003–2016: Trends and Implications

By Kenneth Allen, Phillip C. Saunders, and John Chen

Center for the Study of Chinese Military Affairs
Institute for National Strategic Studies
China Strategic Perspectives, No. 11

Series Editor: Phillip C. Saunders

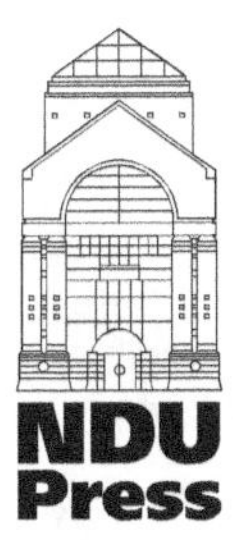

National Defense University Press
Washington, D.C.
July 2017

First printing, July 2017
Printed in the United States of America
ISBN: 978-1977869654

Contents

Illustrations

Figures

Tables

Acknowledgments

The authors thank Alexis Dale-Huang (now with the Carnegie Endowment for International Peace) for research assistance on an earlier draft of the paper. Dr. Joel Wuthnow (National Defense University) and Dr. Michael Glosny (Naval Postgraduate School) provided valuable comments in their peer reviews of the manuscript. An early version of the paper was presented by Ken Allen at the 2014 Council of Advanced Policy Studies–RAND–National Defense University) conference on the People's Liberation Army. Mr. Mark Cozad (RAND), Dr. Bernard Cole (then with the National War College), and Commander Leah Bray, USN (then with the Office of the Secretary of Defense), provided helpful comments on the draft.

Center for the Study of Chinese Military Affairs Research Interns Alex Jeffers, Jordan Link, and Melissa Ladner proofread the manuscript. NDU Press Intern Aidan Low converted the charts and figures for publication.

Executive Summary

China is placing increasing emphasis on military diplomacy to advance its foreign policy objectives and shape its security environment.

- Military diplomacy is part of broader Chinese foreign policy efforts to create a favorable international image, develop soft power, and shape international discourse. Other objectives include shaping China's security environment, collecting intelligence, and learning from advanced militaries.

- The People's Liberation Army (PLA) seeks to forward strategic and operational goals through a variety of interactions with foreign military partners, including senior-level visits, security dialogues, nontraditional security cooperation, military exercises, functional exchanges, and port calls.

- Chinese security cooperation also includes arms sales (conducted by state-owned arms manufacturers), internal security assistance (provided by the Ministry of State Security and Ministry of Public Security), and advice on Internet censorship and control.

Military diplomacy is subordinate to and intended to serve national foreign policy objectives, which determine the relative priority the PLA places on regions and individual countries.

- Military diplomacy is managed in a top-down manner, with the Chinese Communist Party (CCP) Central Committee dictating broad foreign policy goals and the Central Military Commission (CMC) determining specific activities for various parts of the PLA.

- The goal of building stronger bilateral relations with key partners means that the PLA must adapt its planned program of bilateral military activities to accommodate the preferences and constraints of its foreign partners.

- Efforts to shape the security environment can include concealing or downplaying specific military capabilities, highlighting the contributions a stronger PLA can make to regional and global security, and displaying capabilities to deter or intimidate potential adversaries. Since 2010, shaping efforts have placed greater emphasis on displaying capabilities rather than concealing them.

Most PLA diplomatic activity consists of senior-level meetings carried out by the Defense Minister, the Chief of General Staff (now Chief of the Joint Staff), and the Deputy Chief of General Staff (now Deputy Chief of the Joint Staff) who handles foreign affairs and intelligence.

- Senior-level meetings accounted for 83 percent of Chinese military diplomatic activity from 2003 to 2016. China views these meetings as useful for building bilateral relations and providing high-level buy-in for a broader program of military-to-military activities.

- The number of meetings fluctuates in conjunction with the Chinese 5-year political cycle, with visits lowest in years when the CCP changes political and military leaders at a National Party Congress (2002, 2007, 2012).

- Since mid-2010, there has been a significant decline in overseas visits by top PLA leaders. This has been partially offset by the willingness of other countries to ignore protocol and visit China without reciprocal visits from their PLA counterparts.

- Most Chinese military diplomacy is bilateral, but the PLA now participates in a range of multilateral meetings, conferences, exercises, and competitions.

The PLA engages in nontraditional security cooperation with a range of partners to demonstrate that a stronger PLA can play a positive regional security role.

- Most PLA bilateral and multilateral exercises, functional exchanges, and port calls are focused on humanitarian assistance/disaster relief and other nontraditional security activities. Some PLA assets, such as the *Peace Ark* hospital ship, are specifically devoted to these activities.

- Since late 2008, the PLA Navy (PLAN) has maintained a constant presence in the Gulf of Aden to conduct counterpiracy operations. The vessels have also conducted port calls, supported the evacuation of Chinese citizens from Libya and Yemen, and assisted in the disposal of Syrian chemical weapons.

- The PLA has participated in United Nations (UN) peacekeeping operations since 1990 and contributes more troops than any other permanent member of the UN Security Council. PLA participation has expanded from medical and engineering units to include an infantry battalion deployed to South Sudan in 2014.

- China has created a Peacekeeping Training Center near Beijing and has pledged to provide 8,000 troops to participate in a standing UN peacekeeping force.

The PLA has begun to participate in more combat-related exercises and competitions with Russia and Central Asian countries.

- Since 2005, Shanghai Cooperation Organization (SCO) Peace Mission exercises, nominally focused on counterterrorism, have included combat-related activities such as air defense, bombing, and aerial refueling. These are the only exercises where two or more PLA services conduct combined training with foreign partners.

- China's bilateral exercises with Russia focus heavily on combat and combat-support activities. Since 2012, the two navies have conducted a series of exercises in the East China Sea, Mediterranean Sea, and South China Sea that signal their willingness to cooperate in strategically sensitive areas.

- The PLA Army and PLA Air Force have participated in multilateral military competitions hosted by Russia since 2014. This participation reflects growing confidence that the PLA can match international standards.

- The PLA has pushed to engage in "traditional" security cooperation with the U.S. military, but the United States has been reluctant to conduct exercises that might improve PLA combat capabilities.

PLA military diplomacy is focused primarily on major powers such as Russia and the United States and on Asian countries on China's periphery.

- China's most frequent partners are Russia (4.8 percent of all interactions), the United States (4.4 percent), Pakistan (3.9 percent), Thailand (3 percent), and Australia (2.9 percent), all of whom participate in a full range of military diplomatic activities with the PLA.

- PLA military diplomacy places a strong emphasis on Asia, which accounts for 41 percent of all interactions. Southeast Asia (22 percent) and South Asia (9 percent) are higher priority subregions than Northeast Asia (4.8 percent) and Central Asia (5 percent).

- PLA interactions with U.S. treaty allies in Asia have increased since the 2011 U.S. rebalance to Asia and the ascent of Xi Jinping to power in 2012. The PLA has frequent military contacts and a strategic partnership with South Korea but rarely engages the Japanese military.

- The PLA conducts different activities with different partners, sending the most senior-level visits to Asia and Europe, conducting the most military exercises with Russia and SCO nations, and carrying out most of its port calls in the Middle East and Asia.

- The volume of Chinese military diplomatic activity with a particular country generally conforms to the hierarchical priority that the Chinese foreign policy apparatus has assigned to that country.

- China's military interactions with countries under UN sanctions (such as North Korea and Iran before 2016) are limited and not highly publicized.

Military diplomatic activity does not necessarily translate into influence, and many routine activities may not be significant. Activity may reflect the quality of bilateral relations rather than be a means of developing them.

- PLA military diplomacy typically emphasizes form over substance, top-down management, tight control of political messages, protection of information about PLA capabilities, and an aversion to binding security commitments.

- Much of China's military diplomatic activity consists of formal exchanges of scripted talking points in meetings, occasional port calls, and simple scripted exercises focused on nontraditional security issues.

- Most PLA interlocutors are not empowered to negotiate or share their real views, which makes it difficult to build strong personal or institutional ties with foreign counterparts.

- Chinese military relations are also constrained by what activities their foreign counterparts are willing or able to conduct with the PLA.

Military diplomacy can help establish communications and crisis management mechanisms with China and may also encourage Chinese adherence to international rules and norms.

- China's participation in the Western Pacific Naval Symposium contributed to the PLAN's eventual acceptance of the Code for Unplanned Encounters at Sea.

- China uses military diplomacy to build international support for its own preferred rules of behavior, including working with Russia to shape international rules for the space and cyber domains.

Introduction

The international profile of the People's Liberation Army (PLA) has grown significantly over the last half decade, with a notable increase in the frequency and complexity of its activities with partners abroad. As the Chinese military participates in multilateral meetings and engages foreign militaries around the world, it is strengthening diplomatic relations, building the People's Republic of China's (PRC's) soft power, and learning how to deploy and support military forces for longer periods.

Several aspects of the PLA's military diplomacy remain relatively understudied. What are the PLA's objectives in conducting military diplomacy? Which partners does the PLA interact with most? What trends are evident in the pace and type of activities the PLA carries out? Which aspects of PLA military diplomacy should concern U.S. policymakers, and which present opportunities?

This paper employs a variety of sources to analyze overall trends in the PLA's military diplomacy from approximately 2003 to the end of 2016, and it compares trends during the Hu Jintao era to trends since Xi Jinping became chairman of the Central Military Commission (CMC) in November 2012.[1] It uses data collected from a range of primary sources, including Chinese and English articles from *PLA Daily* (解放军报),[2] *PLA Pictorial* (解放军画报), *China Armed Forces* (中国军队),[3] *China Air Force* (中国空军), PRC Chinese and English news services, newspapers, and Web sites (Xinhua, *People's Daily, China Daily, China Military Online*, and the Ministry of National Defense Web site),[4] and China's biennial defense white papers.[5] Western sources include the *China Vitae* Web site, previous writings by the authors, and Andrew Erickson and Austin Strange's book *No Substitute for Experience: Chinese Antipiracy Operations in the Gulf of Aden.*[6]

Our analytic emphasis is on activities where sufficient open source information is available to discern trends and assess PRC motivations. We believe the data we have collected on high-level visits, military exercises, and port calls are fairly complete. However, available data on functional exchanges, dialogues, and military education are much spottier and therefore not incorporated in our quantitative analyses.

This study focuses on PLA military diplomacy and does not address security cooperation carried out by other parts of the Chinese government. These activities include arms sales (conducted by state-owned arms manufacturers), internal security assistance (provided by the Ministry of State Security and Ministry of Public Security), and advice on Internet censorship and control. The study does not attempt a comprehensive assessment of how successful the PLA's military diplomatic efforts have been in achieving the intended objectives.

The study proceeds in four parts. The first section describes the stated and hypothesized objectives underlying the PLA military diplomacy program, outlining a number of military diplomatic activities and how they might correspond to the overall goals of the PLA foreign military relations program. The second section examines trends in PLA military diplomatic activities, examining both the quantitative increase in activity and the increasing diversity of activities the PLA is carrying out. The third section evaluates trends in the PLA's military diplomatic partners, noting which countries interact with the PLA most and in what activities, and compares these findings with China's overall foreign policy orientation. The study concludes by summarizing overall trends in PLA foreign military relations from 2003 to 2016 and considering the broader implications of PLA military diplomacy. (Data on PLA military diplomatic interactions by country are included in the appendix, and the complete dataset is available online at http://ndupress. ndu.edu/Portals/68/Documents/stratperspective/china/PLA-diplomacy-database.xlsx.)

A reorganization in early 2016 instituted major changes to the PLA's structure, including the creation of 15 organizations under the CMC. Specifically, the former General Staff Department is now the CMC Joint Staff Department, the former General Political Department is the CMC Political Work Department, the former General Logistics Department is the CMC Logistic Support Department,[7] and the former General Armament Department is the Equipment Development Department. The PLA also created a separate PLA Army (PLAA) Headquarters, renamed the PLA Second Artillery Force as the PLA Rocket Force and upgraded it from an independent branch to a full service, and created five Theater Commands from the previous seven Military Regions.[8] The 2016 reorganization also placed the office with primary responsibility for coordinating PLA foreign relations (the Ministry of National Defense–Foreign Affairs Office) under the direct supervision of the CMC and renamed it the CMC Office of International Military Cooperation, possibly reflecting Xi Jinping's heightened emphasis on military diplomacy.[9] This paper covers events that occurred before and after the reorganization. The old terms are used for pre-reorganization events; new monikers are used for post-reform events.

PRC Military Diplomacy: Objectives and Means

This section discusses the objectives of Chinese military diplomacy. In addition to objectives explicitly discussed by official and quasi-official Chinese sources, we include additional hypothesized goals in our analysis.

Chinese Objectives

Chinese definitions of *military diplomacy* (军事外交) are broad and encompass a wide variety of activities. A 2007 book by the PLA National Defense University (NDU) Strategy Teaching and Research Department defines military diplomacy simply as "diplomatic activities that are carried out by countries in the realm of military affairs, in service of national defense or military strategy."[10] A more recent definition in the 2011 edition of *PLA Military Terminology* characterizes military diplomacy as the

> *external relationships pertaining to military and related affairs between countries and groups of countries, including military personnel exchange, military negotiations, arms control negotiations, military aid, military intelligence cooperation, military technology cooperation, international peacekeeping, military alliance activities, etc. Military diplomacy is an important component of a country's foreign relations.*[11]

PLA scholars consider a coherent military diplomacy strategy a "necessary part of the national interest," arguing that military relations can "serve as a planning construct for national strategy . . . contain actual or perceived enemies . . . and spur national and military construction."[12] The spectrum of military diplomatic activities is broad, including "military alliances, strategic dialogues, trust-building measures, military negotiations, military intelligence exchanges, military technical cooperation, international military work, border cooperation, international military personnel training, military support activities, military trade, and military academic exchanges."[13]

PLA academicians have ascribed a variety of functions to military diplomacy, drawing distinctions between peacetime, wartime, and crisis functions. During peacetime, military diplomacy "maintains and develops bilateral military security relations . . . provides a platform for handling international security issues . . . molds the country's strategic environment . . . provides a platform to enhance the international influence of the country and the country's military . . . and promotes national defense and military construction."[14] In time of war, military diplomacy serves to "strengthen our alliances and weaken those of the enemy . . . win military aid and material support for combat . . . win international moral and legal support . . . provide a channel to end the war . . . and resolve post-war problems."[15] Crisis applications of military diplomacy include preventing and reducing crises, along with creating, facing, and intensifying crises when necessary or beneficial.[16]

Chinese military diplomatic activities largely conform to the PLA's peacetime conceptions of military diplomacy. Stated objectives are derived from broader PLA missions and include supporting overall national foreign policy, protecting national sovereignty, advancing national interests, and shaping the international security environment. Xi Jinping cited several goals for Chinese military diplomacy in a January 2015 speech to the All-Military Diplomatic Work Conference (全军外事工作会议), including supporting overall national foreign policy, protecting national security, and promoting military construction (for example, military force-building). Xi also highlighted the goals of protecting China's sovereignty, security, and development interests.[17] Academics and scholars reiterate these goals; a lecturer at the PLA Nanjing Political College notes that a major role of Chinese military diplomacy is to "support overall national foreign policy and the new era military strategic direction," and other scholars highlight "shaping the international security environment and promoting military modernization" as additional objectives.[18] Other academics have elaborated further, with one PLA scholar listing the primary goals of military diplomacy as "ensuring national sovereignty and territorial integrity, promoting Chinese military reform, building advantageous international military relations, and safeguarding world peace and stability."[19]

Our analysis also examines unstated goals to provide additional insight into Chinese military diplomacy. Potential goals such as intelligence-gathering, learning new skills and benchmarking PLA capabilities against those of other nations, building partner capacity, and promoting sales of Chinese weapons are typically omitted or only mentioned briefly in Chinese sources on military diplomacy.

Much of the PLA's current military diplomatic activity is focused on protecting and advancing specific Chinese strategic interests.[20] Chinese foreign policy emphasizes managing strategic relations with great powers such as the United States and Russia and engaging countries on China's periphery; Chinese military diplomacy emphasizes interactions with the United States, Russia, and countries in the Asia-Pacific region.[21] China is increasingly dependent on oil and natural gas imported from the Middle East and Africa; the PLA Navy's (PLAN's) counterpiracy presence in the Gulf of Aden facilitates strategic ties in the Middle East and Africa, helps guarantee China's energy security, and provides operational experience in protecting China's sea lines of communication. Xi Jinping's signature foreign policy contribution is the Belt and Road initiative; PLA interactions with militaries in Europe, Africa, Central Asia, and South Asia reinforce this effort.[22]

Chinese military diplomacy objectives can be divided into strategic and operational categories. Strategic objectives employ the PLA as a tool to engage foreign militaries to advance broader Chinese national goals. Strategic objectives include supporting overall PRC diplomacy by engaging key countries and providing public goods, and shaping the security environment by displaying or deploying PLA capabilities. Operational goals are intended to improve the PLA's ability to fight and win wars; these include collecting intelligence on foreign military capabilities and intentions and on potential operating areas, and learning new skills and tactics, techniques, and procedures from other militaries.

Supporting PRC Diplomacy. Military diplomacy supports broader Chinese diplomatic efforts by engaging key countries and providing public goods to enhance China's image. Chinese writings strongly emphasize the PLA's obedience to the Chinese Communist Party (CCP) and by extension view military diplomacy as a tool used to advance larger CCP foreign policy goals.[23] Top-down implementation of Chinese military diplomacy and the broad parameters of this objective mean that nearly all military diplomatic activities are intended to advance wider Chinese diplomatic goals. Senior-level meetings, strategic dialogues, and functional exchanges are often used to deliver diplomatic talking points, nontraditional security operations provide public goods that enhance China's international reputation, and military exercises are often presented as examples of international cooperation.[24]

Shaping the Security Environment. Military diplomacy can also deploy or display PLA capabilities to shape the security environment. The 2015 Defense White Paper calls on the PLA to "develop military-to-military relations . . . and create a security environment favorable to China's peaceful development."[25] Chinese scholars state that shaping a favorable security environment is a crucial mission of military diplomacy, and Chinese media often trumpet the display of PLA capabilities in the defense of national interests.[26] Recent Sino-Russian military exercises in the Mediterranean Sea and South China Sea are intended to show that the strategic partnership between the two countries should be taken seriously by the United States and countries in the Asia-Pacific region.

Collecting Intelligence. Military diplomacy offers opportunities to collect intelligence on foreign capabilities and intentions and on potential operating areas. Chinese sources do not openly mention intelligence-gathering as an objective, but Chinese scholars explicitly warn against revealing secret information during military diplomatic exchanges, a tacit acknowledgment of the intelligence potential of military diplomacy.[27] Nearly all military diplomatic activities can be employed to gather some kind of intelligence because military diplomacy by definition provides some degree of access to foreign militaries. Senior-level meetings and dialogues provide opportunities to collect political intelligence about policy preferences and personnel intelligence about foreign military leaders, functional exchanges and military exercises offer technical intelligence about foreign military capabilities, and naval port calls and nontraditional security operations can be used to collect intelligence about potential operating areas.

Learning New Skills, Tactics, Techniques, and Procedures. Military diplomacy allows the PLA to learn new skills from other countries and benchmark PLA capabilities against those of other nations. Chinese defense white papers consistently emphasize learning from other militaries as a goal of military diplomacy, and quasi-official Chinese sources stress the importance of learning new skills and benchmarking PLA capabilities against those of foreign nations.[28] Chinese scholars emphasize the value of exercises for practicing military skills, and military exercises with foreign partners allow the PLA to compare its capabilities and learn from foreign militaries. Examples include PLA Air Force (PLAAF) participation in Russia's multilateral Aviadarts (航空飞镖) 2014 competition, while Chinese participation in the 2005 Peace Mission (和平使命) exercise helped the PLA learn new skills, with PLAAF fighters refueling from Russian aerial tankers for the first time.[29]

The United States emphasizes the importance of military diplomacy and arms sales in building the capacity of allies and partners and in improving the U.S. military's ability to operate with them in combined and coalition operations.[30] Authoritative Chinese sources do not cite building partner capacity as a goal, but PLA writings identify military aid as an important function of military diplomacy that encompasses the transfers of "weapons, military supplies, technology, and expertise" that can "strengthen political, military, and economic relations between countries."[31] The PLA appears to view building partner capacity as a means of strengthening bilateral relations rather than as an end in itself. Today's more capable PLA has more to teach less advanced militaries. Prominent examples of Chinese military diplomacy that were meant to build partner capacity include the Sino-Pakistani Shaheen (雄鹰) exercises and Chinese military aid to Afghanistan.[32] Chinese writings do not stress building interoperability with partners as an explicit goal of military diplomacy, but this theme is evident in recent combined exercises with Russia.

Categories of Military Diplomatic Activities

These four objectives can potentially be advanced by a range of military diplomatic activities. This section reviews PLA military activities and discusses which goals they support; the results are summarized in table 1.

Table 1. Chinese Military Diplomatic Activities and Objectives

	Strategic Goals		Operational Goals	
	Support PRC Diplomacy	Shape Security Environment	Collect Intelligence	Learn New Skills and Benchmarking
Senior-Level Meetings				
Hosted	x	x	x	
Abroad	x	x	x	
Dialogues				
Bilateral	x	x	x	
Multilateral	x	x	x	
Military Exercises				
Bilateral	x	x	x	x
Multilateral	x	x	x	x
Naval Port Calls				
Escort Task Force	x	x	x	x
Non–Escort Task Force	x	x	x	
Functional Exchanges	x		x	x
Nontraditional Security Operations				
HA/DR	x	x	x	x
PKO	x	x	x	x
MOOTW	x	x	x	x

Senior-Level Meetings. Senior-level meetings involve contact with high-level foreign military or civilian defense leaders, either hosted by the PLA in China or conducted abroad. These meetings support broader Chinese diplomatic efforts to build positive relations with other countries. Chinese writings also credit senior-level meetings with constructing a favorable security environment, protecting regional and global stability, and promoting common development.[33] China's senior military leadership consists of officers at the CMC Vice Chairmen and CMC member-grade levels, supplemented by the Deputy Chief of the CMC Joint Staff Department with responsibility for intelligence and foreign affairs.[34] Since few countries have direct counterparts to the two senior CMC vice chairmen positions, meetings with the CMC Vice Chairmen rather than lower level PLA officers may indicate which countries Beijing prioritizes in military diplomacy. Examining which countries PLA leaders visit and which countries they host can further illuminate priorities. The opportunity costs of overseas travel by senior PLA officers are relatively high, since traveling officers are less able to complete other work, and officers are typically limited to one international trip per year by PLA regulations. Conversely, hosting meetings has a lower opportunity cost, since senior PLA officers can conduct other business while hosting foreign military and defense officials. China has established secure video teleconference links with some countries, such as the United States, that allow senior-level engagements without the need for travel.

Dialogues. The formal nature of high-level dialogues gives these activities an institutional character with different costs and benefits than senior-level meetings. According to the 2015 Chinese Defense White Paper, dialogues are carried out "to promote mutual understanding, mutual trust, and mutual learning."[35] Establishing a bilateral dialogue can signal the importance China places on security relations with another country. Examples include the U.S.-China Strategic and Economic Dialogue and annual PLA bilateral defense strategic dialogues with Australia, France, and Germany.[36] Because bilateral dialogues are typically established on a regular schedule via formal agreements, canceling or not attending a scheduled strategic dialogue may have greater reputational costs than postponing or canceling a bilateral senior-level meeting. Multilateral dialogues allow China to send its desired messages to several countries at once. For instance, hosting the annual Xiangshan Forum and participating in the Shangri-La Dialogue provide China opportunities to shape the regional security agenda and boost its international status.[37]

Military Exercises. Exercises with foreign militaries provide opportunities to learn new skills, benchmark PLA capabilities, gather intelligence on foreign capabilities and intentions, shape the security environment by displaying PLA capabilities, and, in some cases, build partner capacity. A PLA spokesman highlighted these goals in a review of 2014 military diplomacy, stating that the "Chinese armed forces and their foreign counterparts trained together and learned from each other, which boosted mutual trust, deepened cooperation and improved skills. At the same time, the Chinese military gained the opportunity to demonstrate our fine image on the international stage."[38] Bilateral and multilateral exercises can also be used to build partner capacity and a degree of interoperability. Bilateral exercises include the Sino-Pakistani Shaheen (雄鹰) exercise series, and multilateral exercises include the roughly biennial Peace Mission (和平使命) exercises held with Shanghai Cooperation Organization (SCO) nations and intended to build partner counterterrorism capabilities.[39]

Naval Port Calls. These can involve PLAN ships visiting foreign ports or foreign naval vessels hosted by the PLA in China. Chinese sources suggest that port calls provide opportunities for "combined training, mutual understanding, and constructing friendly relations."[40] In the past, the PLAN conducted port calls in conjunction with training deployments or as standalone military diplomacy activities. The counterpiracy patrols in the Gulf of Aden that began in late 2008 have crowded out some of these port calls but have provided new opportunities for port calls by PLAN ships en route to or returning from a counterpiracy deployment.[41] This study distinguishes between port calls conducted as part of an escort task force (ETF/护航编队) and those conducted by other PLAN ships as a non-ETF.[42] Escort task forces typically include three frigates and a replenishment ship, while port calls by non-ETFs can be tailored to specific operational or diplomatic objectives. For example, PLAN submarine port calls in Sri Lanka in 2014 received much attention in the Indian media, while port calls carried out by the PLAN *Peace Ark* hospital ship (和平方舟号医院船) have been viewed as much more benign.[43] The objectives advanced by port calls depend on the ships involved and the activities (such as bilateral exercises) conducted in conjunction with the port call. This study does not include port calls by foreign navies to China or Hong Kong.

Functional Exchanges. These are professional exchanges (including academic and educational exchanges) between PLA and foreign military personnel. Chinese sources emphasize exchanges as a way to build PLA skills, improve friendly ties, and strengthen cooperation, but they also support Chinese diplomatic goals and help gather intelligence.[44] Examples include the PLA National Defense University's educational and exchange programs with multiple countries, PLA academic delegation visits to U.S. military educational facilities, and PLAAF visits with the Portuguese air force that have reportedly included cooperation in personnel training and logistics.[45]

Nontraditional Security Operations. These include a wide variety of military activities that assist a foreign partner or provide public goods to the international community. These include noncombatant evacuations, peacekeeping operations, humanitarian assistance/disaster relief (HA/DR [人道主义援助和灾难救援]) efforts, and antipiracy operations. Chinese writings note the importance of these activities in strengthening PLA capabilities, providing public security goods, and contributing to world peace and development.[46] The latter two objectives support Chinese foreign policy narratives that portray China as a peaceful, responsible great power. Examples include PLAN contributions to the Gulf of Aden antipiracy operation beginning in 2008, PLAAF contributions to the 2014 search for Malaysian Airlines flight MH370, and the PLA Army's 2014 deployment of an infantry battalion to Sudan as part of a United Nations (UN) peacekeeping operation.[47]

PLA Military Diplomatic Activities

While the PLA's aggregate military diplomatic activities have increased in frequency, less attention has been devoted to what activities the PLA is carrying out. Which military diplomatic activities has the PLA emphasized, and which parts of the PLA are involved in executing them? Have these patterns changed since Xi Jinping became CMC chairman in late 2012? If so, are fluctuations in the number and type of military diplomatic activities due to different guidance from Xi?

This analysis groups the PLA's military diplomatic activities into five main categories that broadly parallel the categories described in the first part of the paper:

- senior-level meetings and visits

- international military exercises

- naval port calls

- functional exchanges

- nontraditional security operations, also known as military operations other than war (MOOTW).[48]

This section describes and presents major trends for each category, supplementing qualitative descriptions from Chinese media sources with quantitative data where available.

The data reveal five main conclusions. First, senior-level meetings have fallen in number from their 2010 peak, but still make up the overwhelming majority of military diplomatic interactions. Second, military exercises have increased sharply across all functions and PLA services since Xi Jinping took power. Third, naval port calls have increased in aggregate over time, with ETF port calls largely focusing on replenishment and friendly visits and non-ETF port calls overwhelmingly consisting of friendly visits. Fourth, the PLA has robust academic and functional exchange programs with various countries, although detailed information is lacking. Fifth, the PLA is actively engaged in MOOTW, especially UN peacekeeping operations, participation in naval antipiracy activities, and search and rescue operations at sea.

Senior-Level Meetings and Visits

Overview and Context. The Chinese military views high-level meetings as an important aspect of military diplomacy, and senior PLA leaders devote a significant amount of time to interacting with foreign counterparts. However, senior-level meetings and visits are subject to the constraints and unique characteristics of the PLA. Generally, all senior PLA leaders aside from the Defense Minister and Chief of the General Staff (COGS, now the director of the CMC Joint Staff Department) are limited to one trip abroad per year by regulation, although not every leader takes advantage of the opportunity and exceptions sometimes occur.[49] Senior PLA leaders rarely, if ever, visit the same country twice except to attend multilateral meetings or host the same foreign military leader twice. The Defense Minister does not necessarily host or meet with all his foreign counterparts, who are often hosted by one of the CMC vice chairmen.

The Chinese defense minister has primary responsibility for hosting foreign defense ministers and meeting with other senior foreign military leaders. Other senior PLA officers, including the CMC vice chairmen, the COGS, and the Deputy Chief of the General Staff (DCOGS, now Deputy Chief of the CMC Joint Staff Department) with the foreign affairs and intelligence portfolio also interact regularly with foreign military and civilian officials.[50] However, the defense minister hosts more meetings and travels more than any other senior officer.

Although designated as the counterpart of foreign defense ministers, the Chinese defense minister does not run the Chinese military and is junior to the two CMC vice chairmen. As the military interface between the PLA and the Chinese state, the defense minister is charged with representing military equities and liaising with the State Council in areas of overlapping concern (including foreign policy).[51] Since 2001, travel by four successive defense ministers has increased to attend various defense ministers' meetings, including the SCO annual defense ministers' conferences, the China–Association of Southeast Asian Nations (ASEAN) Defense Ministers' Meeting, and the ASEAN Defense Ministers' Meeting–Plus. Chinese defense ministers typically visit two or three other countries for bilateral talks before or after each multilateral meeting.

The CMC vice chairmen and COGS sometimes stand in for the defense minister at ministerial-level meetings such as the SCO defense ministers' meeting. The DCOGS will also sometimes represent China at international meetings such as the Shangri-La Dialogue in Singapore. The COGS or DCOGS usually represents China during strategic partnerships, dialogues, and consultations instead of the defense minister. The COGS historically averages two trips abroad per year and hosts several foreign military counterparts each year. Only a few of the five to six DCOGS travel abroad and host foreign counterparts.

Visits and meetings by other senior leaders are much more limited. CMC vice chairmen averaged two trips abroad per year to two or three countries from 2009 to late 2012. Historically, the directors of the former General Political Department (now the CMC Political Work Department), the former General Logistics Department (now the CMC Logistic Support Department), and the former General Armament Department (now the CMC Equipment Development Department) have either not traveled or only taken one trip abroad per year. Since the 18th Party Congress in November 2012, the PLAN commander's only travel has been two trips to the United States, while the PLAAF commander has not traveled at all.[52] The PLAN and PLAAF commanders have continued to host several counterparts each year. The commander of the PLA Second Artillery Force (now the PLA Rocket Force), who has few direct foreign counterparts, has not traveled abroad or hosted any visits. Military Region (MR, now Theater Command) commanders occasionally host foreign leaders and travel abroad, but on a similarly limited scale.[53]

A few officers below the grade of theater command leader have opportunities to lead PLA delegations abroad, mostly for service or functional exchanges. For example, in September 2014, the commander of Pacific Air Forces, General Hawk Carlisle, hosted Nanjing Military Region Air Force (MRAF) commander Lieutenant General Huang Guoxian (黄国显) and a seven-member delegation at Pacific Air Forces Headquarters in Hawaii.[54]

Trends in Senior-Level Meetings and Visits. For this study, we identified the names of senior PLA leaders from 2003 to 2016 and tracked the number of meetings and visits they conducted with foreign military counterparts.[55] Each time a senior PLA officer met a foreign military counterpart for a sit-down, face-to-face conversation is counted as a "meeting"; each time a senior PLA officer made a trip abroad from China to another country is counted as a visit.[56] PLA officers can conduct multiple meetings with foreign counterparts on a single internatonal visit.

An examination of the available data yields several observations. First, senior-level meetings represent the overwhelming majority of PLA military-to-military interactions, accounting for 2,174 of 2,799 (or 82.9 percent) total military diplomatic interactions from 1985 to 2016 for which data were available. That percentage decreases somewhat over time as the PLA begins to conduct more naval port calls and international military exercises, but senior-level meetings still represent the bulk of military-to-military interactions. Figure 1 shows total military diplomatic interactions by activity for the years in which meeting data were available.

A likely explanation is the relatively low cost of senior-level meetings compared to the planning, coordination, logistical preparation, and operational expenditure required for other military diplomatic activities. However, one important cost of senior-level meetings is the time

Figure 1. Total Military Diplomatic Interactions by Activity, 2003–2016

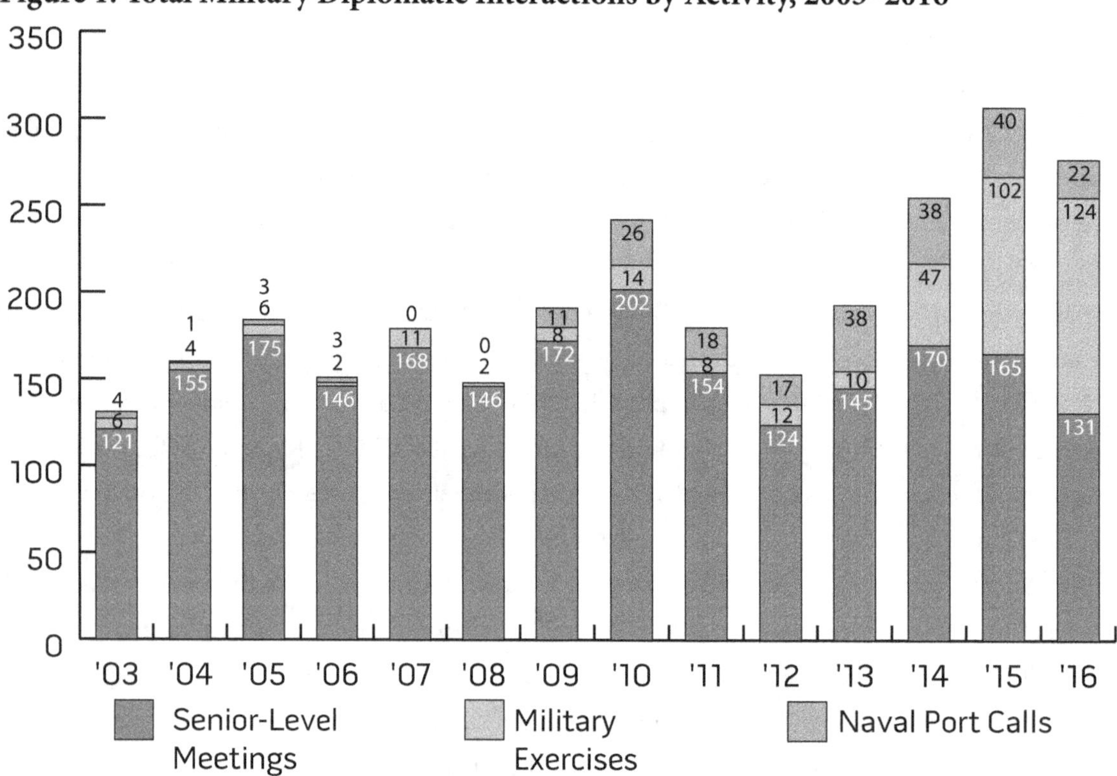

of senior PLA leaders, who are also less able to conduct PLA business while traveling abroad. This suggests a hierarchy of emphasis: meetings abroad have a higher opportunity cost than meetings at home, and meetings with higher level PLA officers are costlier than meetings with lower ranking officials. The implications are addressed in detail in the next section.

Second, the number of senior-level meetings has increased somewhat from 2003 to 2016. The available data show an increase from 121 meetings in 2003 to a peak of 202 meetings in 2010 and a drop to 131 meetings in 2016, with the number of meetings in each year never dropping below the 2003 figure.

Two smaller trends are evident within these data. The first is a cyclical pattern that roughly corresponds with the 5-year Chinese political cycle. Since the late 1970s, China has held party congresses every 5 years. These produce changes in senior political and military leadership, with older leaders retiring and younger ones being appointed. New military leaders took office in late 2002, late 2007, and late 2012 and began to travel and interact with foreign counterparts, with the number of meetings peaking in their third full year in office (in 2005, 2010, and 2015).[57] The years when party congresses are held are characterized by political maneuvering as officials

Figure 2. Total Number of Senior-Level Meetings, 2003–2016

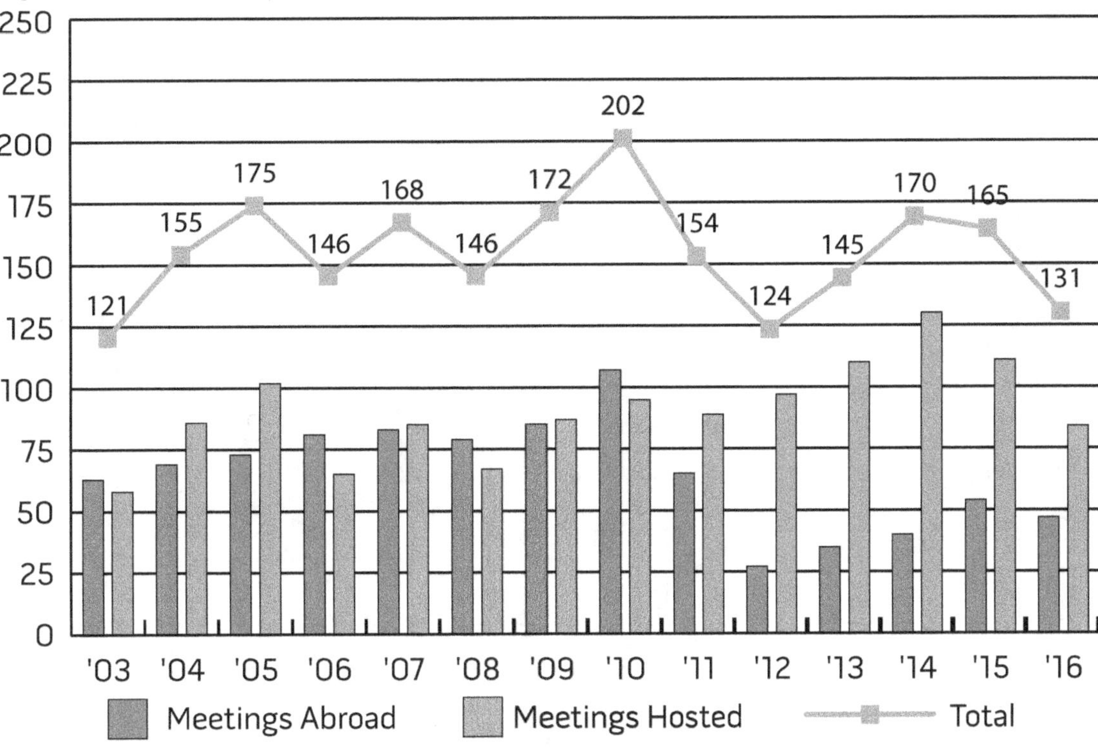

attempt to secure promotions for themselves or their protégés; this produces less interest in traveling and raises the opportunity costs of meeting with foreign counterparts. (The year 2007 is a partial exception to this cyclical pattern but represents a period where the CCP general secretary, premier, and the two CMC vice chairmen all kept their positions.)

A second smaller trend is a significant decline in overseas visits and meetings by senior PLA leaders in 2011 and 2012 after a peak in 2010. Figure 2 documents a steady 28 percent rise in meetings from 2008 to 2010 and a sharp 38 percent decline in meetings from 2010 to 2012. While the increase in meetings in the years leading up to 2010 is modest, the decrease in meetings *abroad* from 2010 to 2012 is especially pronounced, and those figures remain noticeably lower than the numbers from 2003 to 2010. The peak of 107 meetings abroad in 2010 fell to only 27 meetings in 2012, and the 5-year cyclical pattern then restarted from a lower base. Figure 3 shows a sharp drop in both meetings *and* visits abroad, and figure 4 shows that the number of meetings per visit cratered between 2012 and 2014, possibly because most overseas trips were shortened due to austerity and anticorruption campaigns in the PLA. Chinese officers had more

Figure 3. Total Senior-Level Meetings and Visits Abroad, 2003–2016

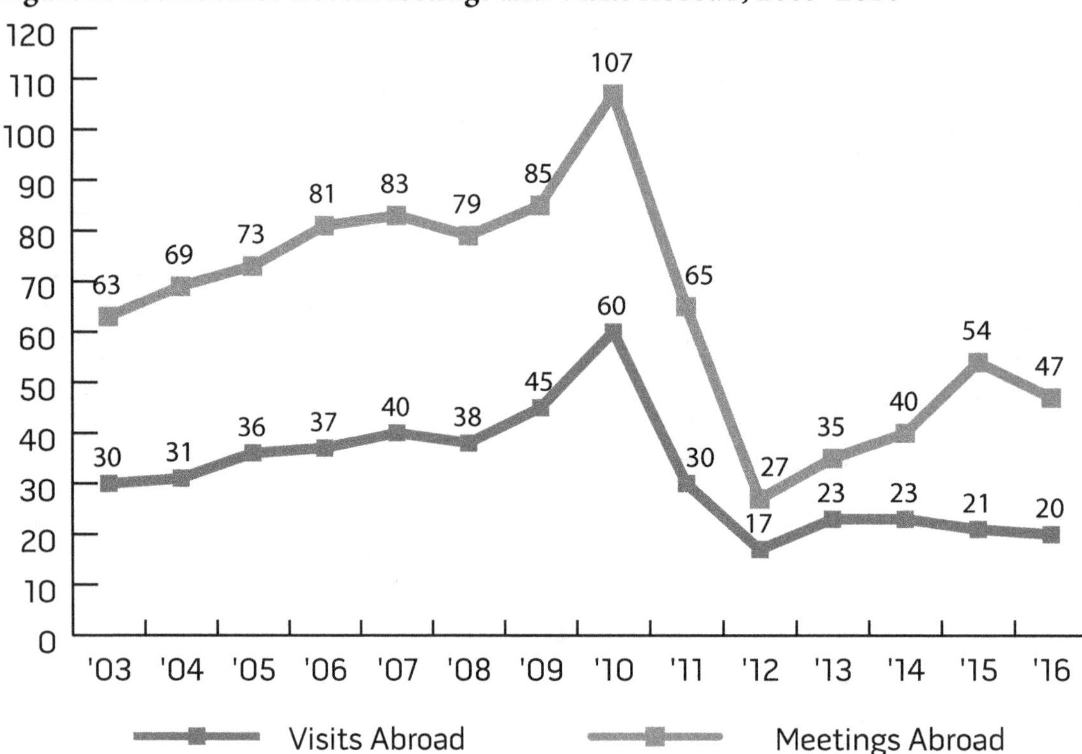

Figure 4. Number of Meetings Held per Senior-Level Visit Abroad

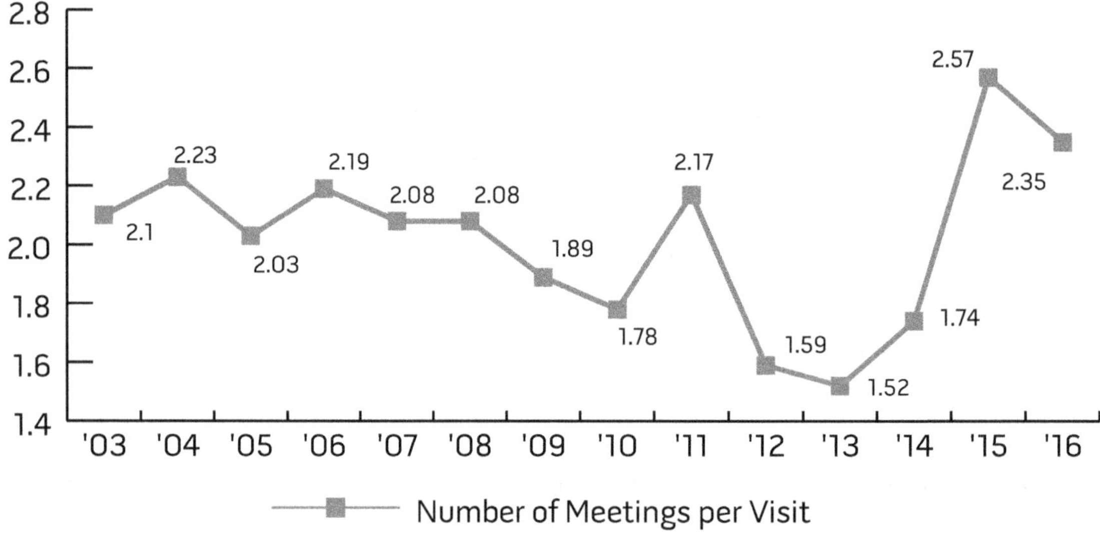

meetings per trip in 2015 and 2016, suggesting some effort to cover more diplomatic ground per trip.

Diplomatic protocol typically requires reciprocity; if one country wants to send a senior leader to visit, it needs to be prepared to host the foreign counterpart in return. The data show that the significant drop in PLA senior leadership travel since 2010 is partially offset by an increase in military meetings hosted by China. This may reflect temporary factors such as the anticorruption campaign, which put pressure on the PLA to reduce both the number and duration of overseas trips.[58] It likely also reflects China's increasing strategic weight; more foreign countries have become willing to disregard protocol and send their senior officers and defense officials to China without reciprocal visits by their Chinese counterparts.

Third, the number of visits hosted and visits abroad fluctuates according to the military relations planning cycle, which usually culminates at the end of the year when each side agrees to

Figure 5. Total Senior-Level Meetings Abroad and Meetings Hosted by Month, 2003–2016

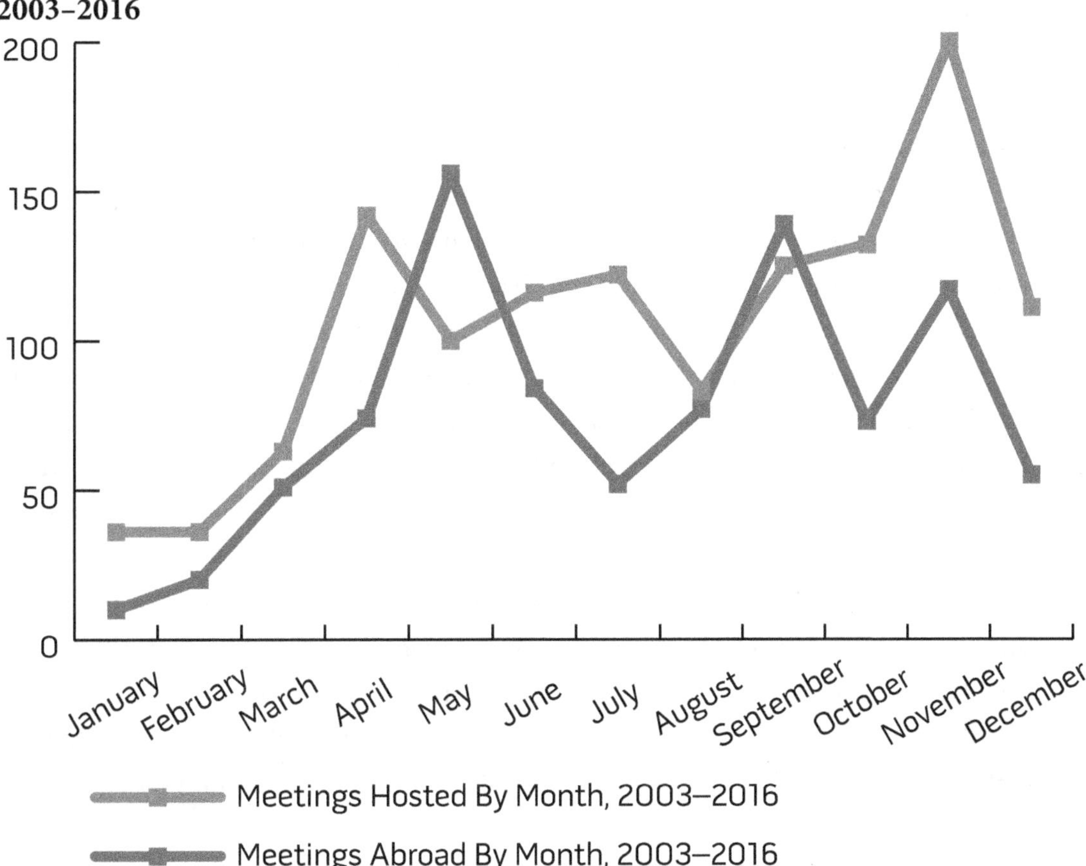

meetings and activities for the next year. Meetings abroad typically spike in May and September and fall dramatically during October for the PRC's National Day and during the Chinese New Year holiday at the end of January and beginning of February. Hosted meetings spike in April and November. Additional factors include winter weather. Very few visits or meetings occur during January through March because of the Chinese New Year holiday.

International Military Exercises

Overview and Context. The PLA has historically been a secretive and somewhat insular organization that was hesitant to engage with foreign counterparts, especially about operational matters. Even when China embraced "reform and opening up" in the late 1970s, the PLA lagged behind other parts of the Chinese government in engaging other militaries. This reticence may have been partly due to fear of revealing military weaknesses or the PLA's inability to meet the standards of advanced militaries. The PLA began conducting bilateral and multilateral "combined exercises" (联合演习) with other countries in 2002. This section gives an overview of the details of these exercises by PLA service participation.

The PLA often refers to combined exercises with other militaries as "joint exercises" (联合演习); this study uses U.S. definitions, which refer to these as "combined exercises."[59] Joint exercises involve the participation of multiple services; participation by multiple branches of a single service is considered a combined arms exercise. Exercises are further categorized by function. Combat activities capture exercises that emphasize combat skills on the high end of the conventional spectrum of conflict, including live-fire drills and combat simulations; combat support activities include communications, engineering, resupply, logistics, survival skills, and fleet navigation and maneuvers; competitions are exercises where the PLA sends forces to compete with those of other nations, typically simulating combat activities; nontraditional security activities include search and rescue, HA/DR, and medical exercises; and antiterrorism exercises are lower intensity, smaller unit activities that resemble conventional combat on the lower end of the spectrum of conflict.

PLA Army International Military Exercises. All the PLA services except for the Rocket Force engage in at least some combined exercises with foreign counterparts, but the PLA Army is the only service to participate in military exercises across all functional categories. The 2012 defense white paper states that combined army training is gradually being increased in breadth and depth.[60] Table 2 shows the distribution of combined exercises by function for all the PLA services.

Table 2. PLA International Military Exercises by Service and Function

	Antiterrorism	Combat	Combat Support	Competition	MOOTW
Army	28 (2)	4 (1)	7 (3)	8 (8)	19 (8)
Navy		14 (1)	50 (17)	1 (1)	22 (6)
Air Force		14 (0)		5 (5)	
Joint		9 (8)	1 (0)	1 (1)	1 (1)

Note: (*X*) indicates the number of multilateral exercises in that category.

Army participation in multilateral exercises emphasizes noncombat activities, such as combat support and MOOTW functions, though the PLA sends only a few personnel at a time to these types of exercises. Notable recent examples include PLAA participation in the U.S.- and Thailand-led multilateral Cobra Gold exercise for the first time in February 2014, in which a total of 17 PLAA soldiers, engineers, and medical personnel, mainly from the Guangzhou MR, participated in HA/DR drills in Thailand.[61] The PLAA also sent 25 personnel from unidentified units (most likely medical and engineering personnel) to a multilateral ASEAN HA/DR exercise that involved 13 countries in April 2014.[62] In October 2014, 10 soldiers from the Australian army, 10 officers and enlisted personnel from the Guangzhou MR, 5 from the U.S. Army, and 5 from the U.S. Marine Corps took part in Kowari 14/Kowary 2014, which focused on survival skills in northern Australia's harsh environment.[63] An additional 100 military personnel provided support in roles including liaison and logistics.

The PLAA participates in bilateral exercises on a broader and more substantive scale. In September 2013, a total of 210 personnel and 26 vehicles participated in the China-Mongolia Prairie Pioneer/Grasslands Vanguard combined HA/DR training event in Tavan Tolgoi, Mongolia. The exercise, focused on rescuing trapped personnel after an earthquake, marked the first time that organic PLA units (rather than hand-picked officers and soldiers) went to Mongolia to take part in combined training.[64] In April 2014, Pakistan hosted the 11-day bilateral combined Peace Angel (和平天使) 2014 HA/DR exercise, with 60 PLA medical personnel participating.[65] This exercise involved setting up a field hospital for 120 personnel after a flood disaster, simulated 26 types of injuries and more than 160 cases of simulated medical treatment tasks for the sick and wounded, and mobilized more than 200 medical and hygienic devices, 10 flights of two types of transport helicopters, and 28 emergency ambulances. China and Pakistan organized related activities, such as academic exchanges, combined tabletop maneuvers, equipment, personnel, and technical training, and a full-personnel and full-equipment drill in preparation for the combined exercise.

Army forces have also begun to participate in military competitions, sometimes with mixed results. The PLA ground forces first participated in an international military competition in August 2014, sending several tanks from the Nanjing MR's 1st Group Army to compete in a four-stage competition dubbed Tank-Biathlon 2014 (坦克兩項-2014) at the Alabino Training Range near Moscow.[66] The competition included a single-tank obstacle course that called for tanks to negotiate water, mine fields, soil ridges, and cliffs while completing various shooting subjects on the way, along with short-distance and speed competitions, physical competitions, and a relay race, in which the four best-performing teams from the previous three stages competed with each other. China was the only nation to use an indigenously produced tank, the Type-96A (ZTZ-96A), while the remaining 11 countries competed in Russian T-72B tanks. The Chinese decision proved disastrous—the Chinese tank suffered from poor mechanical reliability throughout the competition. The lead tank's caterpillar track fell off during the final stage and the vehicle stalled in front of the crowd, allowing a Russian T-72B to overtake it and beat it to the finish line. The Chinese team finished third overall, behind Russia and Armenia.

PLA Navy International Military Exercises. The PLAN participates in the most international combat exercises of all the PLA services but thus far has not participated in an international military competition. Its exercise interactions are largely focused on combat, combat support, and MOOTW functional categories. According to the 2012 Defense White Paper, combined bilateral and multilateral maritime exercises and training are being expanded.[67]

The PLAN's first international exercises were relatively simple search and rescue exercises (SAREXs), but the PLAN has gradually increased the complexity of these exercises and incorporated them as parts of larger and more demanding exercise interactions. The PLAN now routinely includes SAREXs and HA/DR drills in its combined exercises as well as during various port calls. For example, in September 2013, the PLAN and the U.S. Navy held a SAREX near Hawaii, the first such exercise in 7 years.[68] The exercise involved 1,000 personnel and was carried out by the PLAN guided-missile destroyer *Qingdao*, guided-missile frigate *Linyi*, and a helicopter. U.S. Navy participants included the guided-missile cruiser USS *Lake Erie*, an auxiliary ship, and two helicopters. The exercise included the first helicopter formation flight, first establishment of a joint damage control team, and first search of the same waters by air forces. The SAREX, which was commanded by the two navies in turn, involved four stages featuring nine areas. Activities included "formation flight communications and commands, joint missile-helicopter searching for distressed ships, rescues of ships in distress, and ship formation movements."[69]

PLAN multilateral exercises typically focus on noncombat activities, sometimes because foreign partners are reluctant to practice combat with the Chinese navy. For instance, the PLAN participated in the U.S.-sponsored Rim of the Pacific (RIMPAC) 2014 exercises, sending the missile destroyer *Haikou*, missile frigate *Yueyang*, comprehensive supply ship *Qiandaohu*, and hospital ship *Peace Ark*, as well as two helicopters, a commando unit, and a diving squad, totaling 1,100 officers and soldiers.[70] The PLAN also deployed an uninvited *Dongdiao*-class auxiliary general intelligence ship to monitor the exercise, highlighting the utility of international military exercises for intelligence-gathering.[71] China sent a similar vessel to monitor the RIMPAC exercise in 2012. U.S. exercise organizers were careful to keep China out of combat-related activities because the participation of Chinese navy personnel might violate the restrictions in the National Defense Authorization Act of 2000.[72] China did participate in "simple" gunnery exercises that involved shooting at a target in the sea, providing an opportunity for U.S. Navy officers to assess the accuracy of Chinese gunnery. The PLAN also participated in RIMPAC 2016, including in a submarine rescue tabletop exercise and a field exercise to test the compatibility of the PLAN undersea rescue vehicle with the rescue seating surfaces on Western submarines.[73] The PLAN has participated in several HA/DR events in conjunction with port calls and other military exercises—for instance, in April 2014, the PLAN's *Changbaishan* amphibious landing ship from the South Sea Fleet joined vessels from 13 other countries in Indonesia's Komodo (科摩多) HA/DR combined exercise.[74]

The PLAN's most complex bilateral exercises are the Maritime Cooperation (海上联合) exercise series with the Russian navy, which includes comparatively demanding combat-related activities.[75] The 2012 iteration near Qingdao included combined air defense, maritime replenishment, combined antisubmarine warfare, combined search and rescue, and rescue of a hijacked ship, as well as sea-to-sea, sea-to-underwater, and sea-to-air live-fire practice. The 2013 exercise in the Sea of Japan involved 18 ships from both sides performing similar activities. The PLAN deployed four destroyers, two frigates, one comprehensive replenishment ship, three helicopters, and one special operations detachment, the Chinese navy's single largest overseas deployment for exercises with a foreign country. The 2014 version included joint verification and identification for use in the Chinese-declared air defense identification zone in the East China Sea and also featured free combat without a preplanned scenario, a first for any PLA service in a combined exercise. For the first time, vessels from both sides maneuvered in mixed Chinese-Russian formations against an opposition force, with the detection and communication devices on all warships and aircraft operating simultaneously, thus reflecting a high level of trust.[76]

Sino-Russian combined naval exercises are increasingly used to shape the international security environment. The 2014 exercise coincided with President Vladimir Putin's visit to China on May 20–21, and both Putin and Xi cited the exercise as an illustration of Sino-Russia strategic cooperation.[77] In May 2015, the two navies conducted their annual naval exercise in the Mediterranean Sea, demonstrating the ability to project power and showcasing the relevance of Sino-Russian security cooperation for issues such as Syria.[78] In September 2016, the exercise was conducted in the northern part of the South China Sea near Hainan Island. The exercise followed an international tribunal ruling in July 2016 that found many of China's maritime claims in the South China Sea to be unjustified under the UN Convention on the Law of the Sea. Though both Russian and Chinese interlocutors denied that the maneuvers were being targeted at any third party, the timing and location of the drills were not lost on observers. Moreover, the exercise included extensive joint antisubmarine warfare drills and a joint amphibious landing exercise involving 90 Russian and 160 Chinese marines.[79] PLA scholars have noted explicitly that one of the main purposes of naval diplomacy is to protect national territorial integrity.[80]

PLA Air Force Combined Exercises. The PLAAF has also increasingly become involved in bilateral and multilateral exercises with foreign air forces.[81] According to a PLAAF spokesman, "The PLA Air Force has adopted a more outspoken and active attitude to reach out in the past several years to demonstrate the force's combat prowess. It has actively participated in a host of multinational drills, trainings, and exchange activities, thus gaining a lot of useful experience that has been adopted to improve the combat capabilities of our commanders and pilots."[82]

Exercises allow the PLAAF to demonstrate its improving capabilities to the international community, observe and learn from foreign militaries in an operational environment, and serve as a vehicle for building trust and solidifying security cooperation with select countries. Units involved have included fighters, multirole, attack, bomber, and transport aircraft, as well as airborne troops. All the deployments have been supported by Il-76 transports, and some have involved aerial and/or ground refueling en route.

PLAAF participation in Peace Mission joint exercises has included many "firsts." PLAAF fighters refueled from Russian tankers for the first time in 2005, the PLAAF deployed domestically produced new weapons abroad for the first time in 2007, and it conducted a low-altitude entry and used precision-guided missiles to attack a camouflaged ground target in 2009. The PLAAF deployed J-10s and H-6s from China with support from airborne early warning and tanker aircraft that operated within China, were escorted by foreign aircraft after crossing the border, and conducted a ground attack on foreign soil under informatized and complex electromagnetic environment conditions in 2010. The 2014 Peace Mission exercise marked the deployment of the most weapons and equipment for any exercise, including a total of 23 aircraft (seven different variants including fighters, attack aircraft, airborne early warning aircraft, transports, and unmanned aerial vehicles), as well as airborne, communications, and radar troops.

The PLAAF has also begun to conduct bilateral exercises with other partners. Examples include PLAAF Su-27s that participated in Turkey's 2010 Anatolian Eagle (安纳托利亚之鹰) exercise and PLAAF J-11 fighters that conducted combined training and aerial maneuvers in Pakistan's Shaheen-1 (雄鹰-1) exercise in March 2011.[83] In September 2013, the PLAAF hosted Pakistan for Shaheen-II and flew J-10s during the exercise,[84] and the PLAAF returned to Pakistan for Shaheen-III in May 2014.[85]

PLAAF airborne troops began participation in bilateral exercises in 2011. PLAAF airborne troops participated in the Cooperation (合作) 2011 urban combined antiterrorism training in October 2011 in Venezuela. In July 2011 and November 2012, airborne troops participated in Divine Eagle (神鹰), which has also been identified as Condor and Swift Eagle, with Belarussian airborne forces in Belarus and China, respectively.[86] The airborne forces visited Indonesia for the Sharp Knife (利刃) drills in November 2013 and hosted Indonesia's airborne forces for the Sharp Knife Airborne–2014 antiterrorism drill in October 2014.[87] In May 2014, Russian airborne troops visited the PLAAF's Airborne Troop College (空军空降兵学院) in Guilin to exchange views and become familiar with the college's training and facilities.[88] Though these exercises are often billed as "antiterrorism" drills, the content of the exercises suggests that the units involved are practicing skills closer to traditional combat activities, which is how they are coded in this study's data.

The PLAAF has also begun participating in international military competitions. One of the most significant events occurred July 22–28, 2014, when the Russian air force hosted Aviadarts (航空飞镖) 2014 at Voronezh, Russia, which included the PLAAF and Belarus air force.[89] Two PLAAF Su-30s and four pilots competed in six separate events aimed at showing pilot skills in visual reconnaissance, navigation, single-plane or two-plane aerobatics, and air-to-ground attacks.[90] They launched 24 rockets and fired 60 cannon rounds. Based on the total scores, Russia took first place, China took second, and Belarus third. An Il-76 accompanied the aircraft to Russia. The PLAAF has continued to participate in subsequent Aviadarts competitions.

Joint International Military Exercises. PLA joint exercises (involving multiple services) with foreign militaries are almost always in multilateral settings. The few bilateral exercises are the 2013 iteration of the Peace Mission exercises conducted with Russia, the Peace and Friendship 2014 joint tabletop exercise with Malaysia, and the Joint Sea 2015 maritime exercises with

Russia. The 2005 and 2009 iterations of the Peace Mission exercises involved only Chinese and Russian participants but were planned and executed as multilateral events with SCO observer nations in attendance.

Most PLA joint exercises involve combat activities, and Peace Mission joint exercises have increased in complexity over time. Despite their "antiterrorism" billing, the Peace Mission exercises involve extensive conventional combat activities. For instance, Peace Mission 2009 involved sophisticated weapon systems, including surface-to-air missiles;[91] Peace Mission 2010 included PLAAF J-10 multirole aircraft and H-6 bombers that conducted air-to-ground attacks.[92] Peace Mission 2013 was especially oriented toward conventional combat operations, involving 646 PLA personnel, tanks, armored personnel carriers, light reconnaissance vehicles, 120mm self-propelled howitzers, 152mm self-propelled guns, five JH-7A fighter-bombers, and helicopters. The primary ground force organizations included the 190th Mechanized Brigade, a special operations forces (陆军突击分队) brigade, and an army aviation regiment. A total of 600 Russian military personnel participated in the three-phase exercise, which included force projection and deployment, campaign planning, and campaign implementation.[93] The 2014 iteration was the largest Peace Mission exercise to date and marked the first time that China served as the chief director of a combined military exercise. The drill simulated an SCO military response, at the invitation of a host nation, to an extremist or separatist group from abroad that was inciting people to join a terrorist insurgency in the SCO host nation. The PLA ground force included Z-19 and Z-10 helicopters. The PLAAF sent 23 aircraft of seven types including J-10, J-11, and JH-7 fighters and attack aircraft, as well as KJ-200 early warning aircraft and several combat vehicles from the airborne forces. The exercise also included more information technology and information-based warfare. It was the first time that the Chinese military assigned reconnaissance-strike integrated unmanned aerial vehicles to participate in a combined exercise.[94]

The increased complexity of joint exercises has sometimes led to poor outcomes. One report from the *Moscow Times* indicated that inaccurate maps led to approximately 15 Russian and 60 Chinese deaths during Peace Mission 2009.[95] Preparation time for that combined exercise was shortened from 10 months in the previous exercises to 4 months.

Peace Mission joint exercises have increased in frequency and typically involve larger numbers of PLA personnel. Peace Mission exercises have been held in 2005, 2007, 2009, 2010, 2012, 2013, 2014, and 2016, with SCO nations acting either as active participants or as observers. Most of these exercises involve larger numbers of PLA personnel from various PLA services—the smallest Peace Mission exercise in 2012 involved some 369 personnel from the PLA, while the largest in 2005 included about 8,000 PLA personnel.[96]

Overall Trends in International Military Exercises. This study identifies all PLA participation in international military exercises in available media reporting and tracks the total number of exercises and the number of interactions that the PLA had with foreign militaries during these exercises.[97] An examination of the available data yields five notable findings.

First, PLA participation in international military exercises has increased dramatically since its first exercise in 2002. Figure 6 shows both the overall increase and an especially pronounced increase from 2014 to 2016, with the number of exercises almost quadrupling from 8 in 2013 to 30 in 2014.

The increase in international military exercises highlights the PLA's emphasis on using military exercises as a tool to engage with foreign militaries.[98] The PLA's willingness to take part in increasingly complex exercises also reflects its growing confidence in its own capabilities. Despite the occasional instances of equipment failure, official media reports claim that exercises are opportunities "during which a range of advanced weapons, tactics and operational methods were unveiled, fully demonstrating the openness and confidence of the PLA."[99] The increased participation may also reflect a greater propensity to use international military exercises to shape China's security environment. A Ministry of National Defense (MND) spokesman noted that military exercises gave the Chinese military "the opportunity to demonstrate our fine image on the international stage."[100] China and Russia have used combined naval exercises in

Figure 6. Total PLA International Military Exercises, 2002–2016

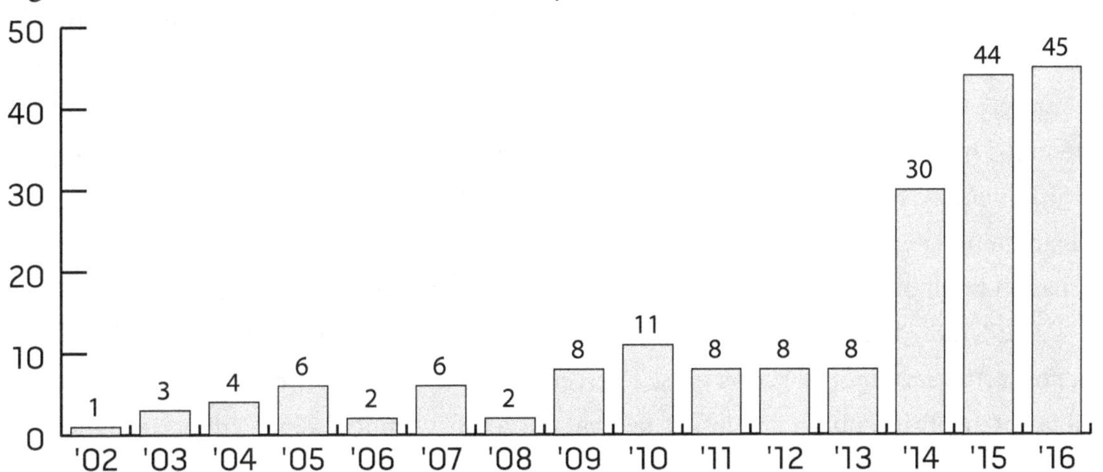

Figure 7. Total PLA International Military Exercises by Type, 2002–2016

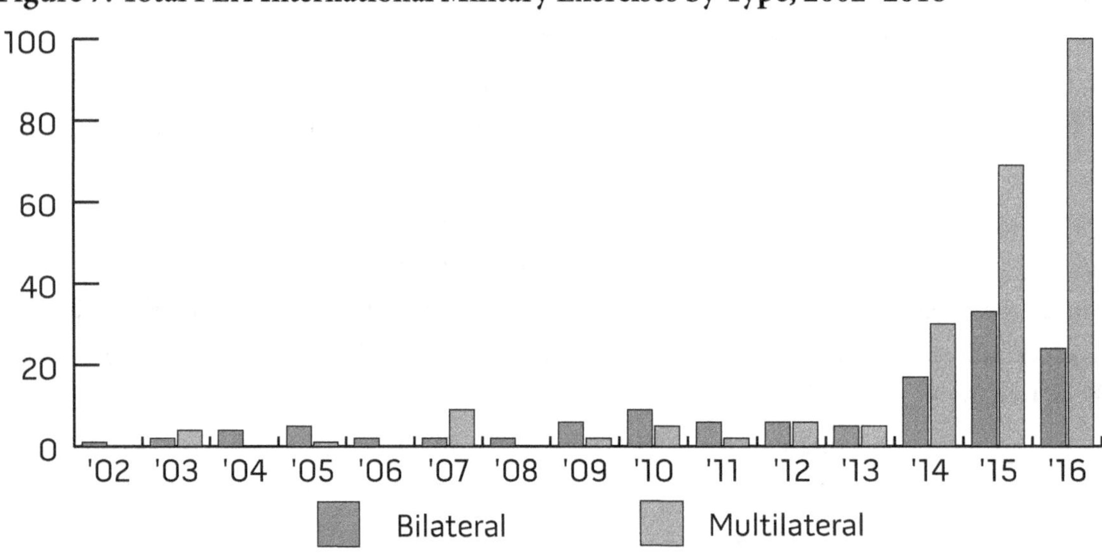

sensitive regions such as the East China Sea, Mediterranean Sea, and South China Sea to demonstrate their strategic cooperation and to reinforce each other's diplomatic efforts.[101]

Second, the PLA has increasingly favored multilateral exercises in recent years. Figure 7 shows a sharp increase in multilateral international military exercises between 2014 and 2016, which reflects not only an emphasis on multilateral engagement but also a trend toward exercises with more nations per event. Much of the increase in multilateral exercises beginning in 2014 can be attributed to increased Chinese participation in international military competitions.

The PLA's increased emphasis on multilateral military exercises may reflect increased efforts to shape foreign perceptions. Sustained contact with one partner during a bilateral exercise provides a better opportunity for the PLA to learn. Multilateral exercises are more complicated to organize but have a larger audience, making them better vehicles for demonstrating peaceful intentions by engaging in nontraditional security cooperation or for shaping China's security environment by displaying capabilities to a wider audience. China helps organize the Peace Mission multilateral exercises, but much of the increase in numbers is attributable to PLA participation in multilateral exercises, especially military competitions organized by Russia.

Third, more than half of all PLA international military exercises involve combat or combat support activities. Figure 8 shows that 22 percent of the exercises between the PLA and foreign militaries involve combat activities, 31 percent are combat support, 8 percent occur in military skills competitions, and 16 percent are antiterrorism exercises. Put another way, only 23 percent

Figure 8. Total PLA International Military Exercises by Function, 2002–2016

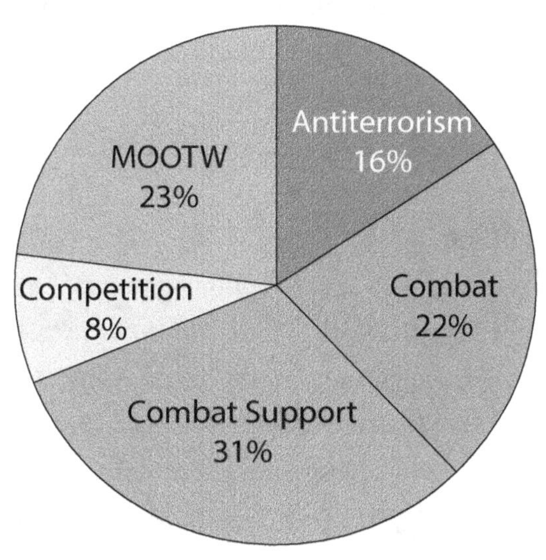

of the military exercise interactions are focused on MOOTW. Figure 9 illustrates increases in numbers of military exercises in all functional categories, though MOOTW and antiterrorism exercises appear to fall off after 2014 as the PLA has become more willing to emphasize its increasing combat capabilities.

Increases in military exercises across all categories, especially in combat and combat support activities, seem to validate Chinese claims that PLA participation in international military

Figure 9. Total PLA International Military Exercises by Function, 2002–2016

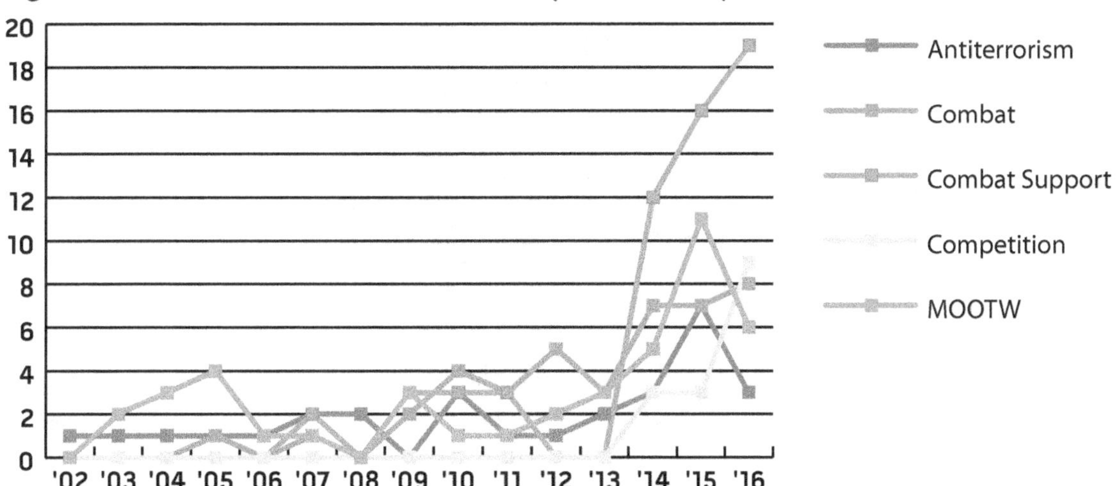

exercises is "increasingly shifting from nontraditional security to traditional security and are more real combat oriented."[102] This likely reflects an increased PLA ability and desire to learn combat and combat support skills from other militaries, but it may also reflect the leadership's desire to use military exercises to shape China's security environment. It also indicates that China feels less need to discuss its increasing military capabilities only in the context of nontraditional security issues.

Fourth, the PLAA and PLAN conduct the overwhelming majority of international exercises, with the PLAAF only accounting for a small fraction of exercise participation and the Rocket Force conspicuously absent. Figure 10 shows that army-to-army and navy-to-navy exercises account for 83 percent of international military exercises, while air force exercises comprise only 10 percent of the total, and the Rocket Force does not participate at all. Figure 11 illustrates the PLAAF's late entry into the realm of international military exercises. The PLAAF held its first international military exercise in 2010 with Turkey, 8 years after other PLA services began exercising with foreign militaries.

What explains the variation in service participation in international military exercises? The late start to air force participation could reflect efforts to maintain secrecy about capabilities or budget constraints on the maintenance and logistics funds required to fly PLAAF aircraft to other countries. Alternatively, the air force may simply have not felt confident enough to send

Figure 10. Total PLA International Military Exercises by Service, 2002–2016

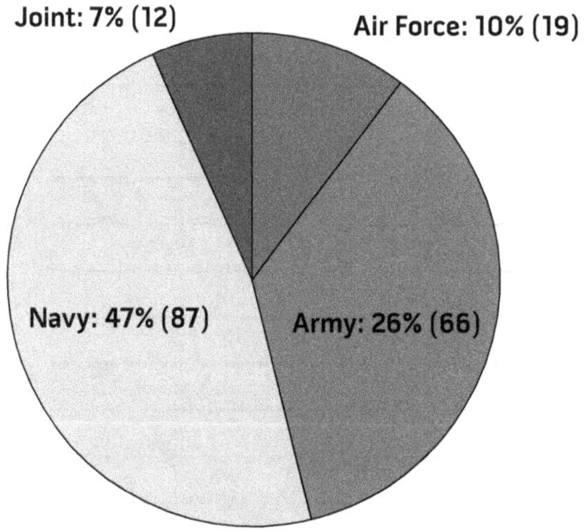

Figure 11. Total PLA International Military Exercises by Service over Time, 2002–2016

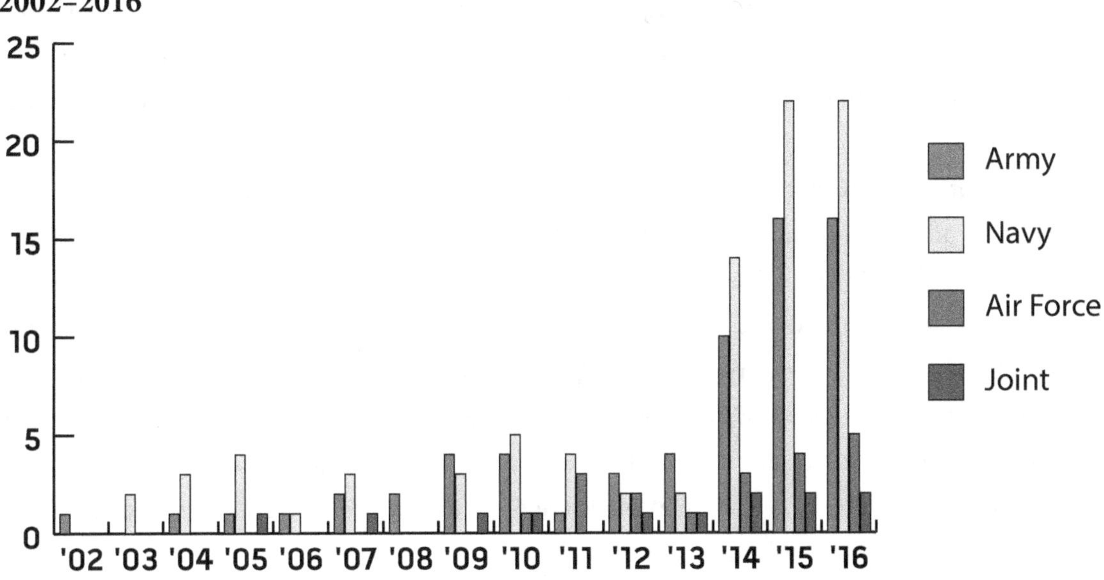

pilots and aircraft to participate in exercises with other countries until they reached a certain level of proficiency. The Rocket Force's conspicuous absence likely reflects its lack of genuine foreign counterparts and the sensitivity of nuclear operations.

Fifth, the PLA rarely participates in truly joint military exercises with foreign militaries. Figure 11 shows that joint military exercises in which more than one PLA service participates in events with foreign militaries occur only intermittently. Joint exercises have gradually increased in frequency, occurring annually since 2012 and only increasing to two events per year starting in 2014. Prior to 2014, *all* of these joint military exercises were Peace Mission events held in co-operation with SCO countries. The increases from 2014 to 2016 can be attributed to non–Peace Mission exercises, such as a joint tabletop exercise with Malaysia in 2014 code-named Peace and Friendship 2014, participation in Russian-held International Military Games and the second half of the Joint Sea naval maneuvers in 2015, and the ASEAN HA/DR 2016 exercises. None of the net increases in joint military exercises from 2014–2016 involve combat activities.

Naval Port Calls

Overview and Context. From 1985 to 2008, the PLAN typically conducted only a handful of port calls per year, most of which were "friendly visits" that did not involve much operational interaction with the host-nation's navy. The PLAN's ongoing participation in counterpiracy deployments in the Gulf of Aden since late 2008 generated new requirements for port calls (for ships in the antipiracy ETFs to replenish supplies) and provided new opportunities for these ships to conduct friendly visits to foreign ports. The operational requirements of deploying and sustaining ETFs crowded out port calls by PLAN ships other than the *Peace Ark* hospital ship from 2009 to 2012; other non-ETF port calls resumed in 2013. This section discusses both types of port calls.

Port Calls and Activities of Antipiracy Escort Task Forces. PLAN ETFs conduct two types of port calls. Replenishment visits usually last 2 to 5 days, during which the vessels receive fuel, fresh water, vegetables, and fruits.[103] Crews are usually met by the Chinese ambassador and military attachés, but the vessels are not open for public display and the crew does not interact with the host-country's navy. Friendly visits generally last 2 to 4 days, with the crew usually met by the Chinese ambassador and military attachés, as well as host-country government and naval officials.[104] Chinese expatriates and students in the country attend welcoming and departure ceremonies. Throughout the visit, the vessels are open to the public. PLAN crewmembers also play basketball or soccer with the host navy.

Key personnel from some antipiracy ETFs have visited foreign escort task forces, and foreign task force personnel have also visited PLAN vessels. For example, on May 4, 2013, Rear Admiral Yuan Yubai (袁誉柏), who served concurrently as commander of ETF-14 and as a North Sea Fleet (NSF) deputy commander, hosted the commander of Combined Task Force 151 on the *Harbin* destroyer.[105] In June 2014, Rear Admiral Huang Xinjian (黄新建), who served concurrently as commander of ETF-17 and as an East Sea Fleet deputy chief of staff, led a six-member delegation to visit the Singaporean guided-missile frigate RSS *Tenacious*.[106] ETF-17's command vessel *Changchun* also hosted the commander of the European Union's 465 Task Force in July 2014.[107]

Some ETFs participate in combined maritime exercises while deployed. For example, in September 2012, ETF-12 conducted the first combined counterpiracy exercise with the United States, and in August 2013 ETF-14 conducted the second exercise between the two navies.[108] On March 4, 2013, Pakistan organized the Peace-13 (和平-13) multinational maritime combined military exercise that involved vessels from 14 countries and special operations forces from 7 countries, including China's ETF-14 and vessels from the United States, United Kingdom, and Japan.[109] During May and June 2014, ETF-16 held bilateral antipiracy combined drills in the Gulf of Guinea with Nigeria's navy and Cameroon's navy.[110] These were the first antipiracy drills between the navies, as well as the PLAN's first maritime drills in the Gulf of Guinea with a foreign navy. On March 20, 2014, ETF-16 also conducted the PLAN's first combined antipiracy drill with a European Union combined task force, which comprised vessels from France, Germany, and Spain.[111] Finally, during a port call in Iran in September 2014, the ETF-17's *Changchun* destroyer and *Changzhou* frigate conducted "unprecedented combined naval drills in the strategic Persian Gulf."[112]

Port Calls and Activities of Non–Escort Task Force Ships. Regular navy warships have continued to conduct port calls after ETFs began regularly deploying to the Gulf of Aden after 2009, although only the hospital ship *Peace Ark* made overseas port calls from 2009 to 2012. In 2013, three PLAN vessels (the guided-missile destroyer *Lanzhou*, guided-missile frigate *Liuzhou*, and comprehensive supply ship *Poyanghu*) from the South Sea Fleet conducted the PLA's first passage through the Magellan Strait, making port calls in Argentina, Brazil, and Chile.[113] One especially notable port call occurred in September 2014, when a Type-039 (*Song*-class) conventional submarine (hull number 329) from the South Sea Fleet visited Sri Lanka along with the NSF's *Changxinghu* comprehensive supply ship.[114] The submarine also deployed to the Gulf of Aden, where it supported the 18th ETF for an undetermined period.[115] The limited utility of a submarine for antipiracy operations suggests other motivations for both the port call and submarine deployment, including practicing subsurface warfare in distant waters and shaping the regional security environment.

Training vessels also pay port calls to foreign countries as part of PLAN diplomatic efforts. The PLAN's only officer cadet training ship, the *Zhenghe* (郑和号训练舰), has been an especially prolific traveler since it became operational and was assigned to the Dalian Naval Ship Academy (part of the North Sea Fleet) in April 1987.[116] Since its first port call to the United States (Hawaii) in 1989, it has visited at least 25 different countries, including multiple visits to several countries, and sailed over 300,000 nautical miles.[117] The *Zhenghe* routinely welcomes foreign military cadets as part of its friendly port calls: journeys in 2012, 2013, and 2014 welcomed cadets from both various PLAN academies as well as maritime students from India, Myanmar, Indonesia, Vietnam, and others. The *Zhenghe*'s 2014 voyage, conducted with the guided-missile frigate *Weifang* (潍坊舰), featured exchanges at the Indonesian Naval Academy and welcomed students from Australia, New Zealand, Singapore, Thailand, and Bangladesh.[118] While visiting Indonesia, the PLAN task force and the Indonesian navy's Patrol Ship 813 conducted a combined exercise in the Java Sea. The exercise included task force maneuvering, communications, and employing the Code for Unplanned Encounters at Sea, a first for the PLAN in a combined exercise.

The *Peace Ark* hospital ship has also been active in port calls and medical assistance missions abroad. The ship, commissioned in 2008, made a number of port calls during Harmonious Mission overseas deployments to Africa (2010), the Caribbean (2011), Southeast Asia (2013),

Figure 12. Total Outbound Naval Port Calls, 1985–2016

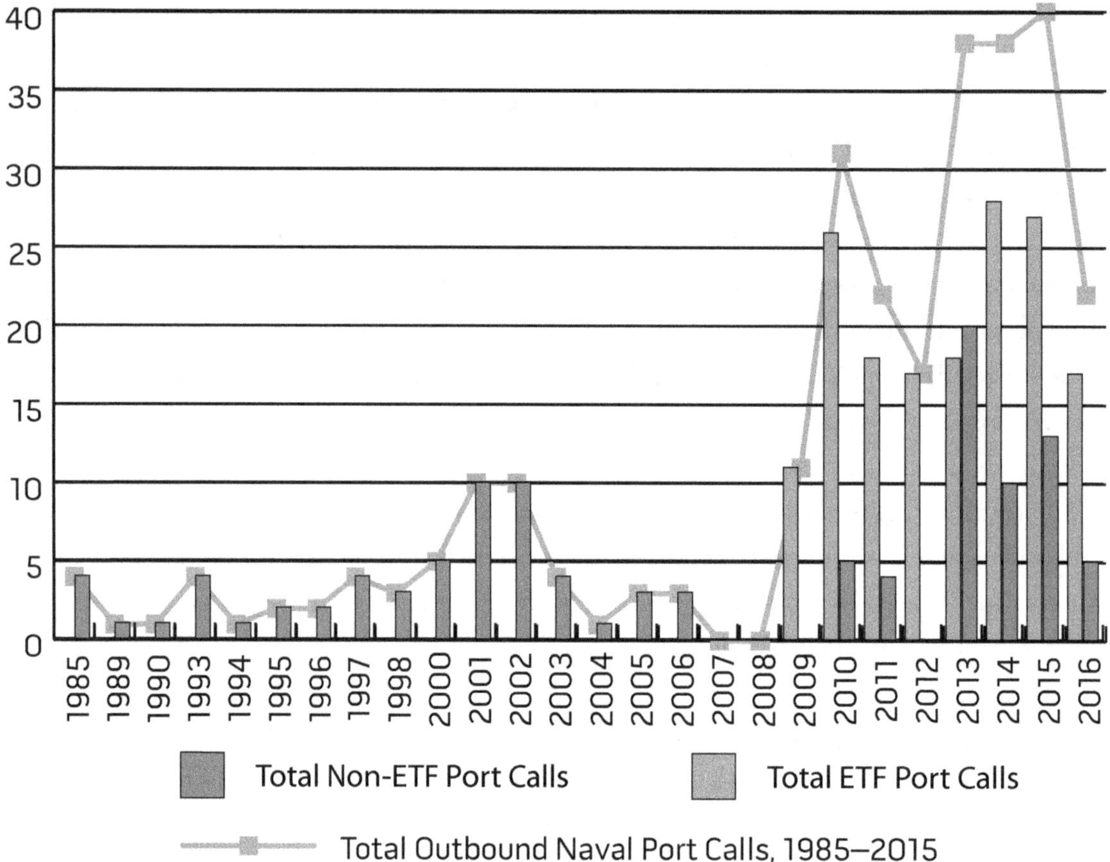

the South Pacific (2014), and Central America and the Caribbean (2015). The *Peace Ark*'s port calls represented the only non-ETF port calls made by the PLAN from 2009 to 2012.

Overall Trends in Naval Port Calls. For this study, we identified all PLA naval port calls in available media reporting and grouped them by function, fleet, and time. Some port calls were conducted by task forces comprised of ships drawn from all three PLAN fleets—these were grouped as "all," while those port calls conducted by unknown ships from unknown fleets were grouped as "unknown." Some uncertainty exists as to exactly which port calls were carried out by which ETF, as some port calls occurred when two ETFs were on station. This uncertainty is reflected in the data labels for each ETF.

The available data reveal several notable observations. First, the aggregate number of naval port calls has increased significantly since the PLAN conducted its first port call in 1985. Figure 12 shows that the PLAN did not conduct any port calls in 2007 and 2008 and that the operational requirements of deploying and sustaining ETFs crowded out port calls by PLAN ships other than the *Peace Ark* from 2009 to 2012. The PLAN resumed port calls by other non-ETF ships in 2013, and the number of these port calls has been higher than the historical level from 1985 to 2008.

Second, port calls are split mostly evenly by fleet. However, voyages by training vessels account for the higher number of port calls from North Sea Fleet ships, while the East Sea Fleet has made most of the antipiracy port calls. Approximately 43 percent of non-ETF port calls are carried out by the North Sea Fleet, 33 percent by the East Sea Fleet, and 19 percent by the South Sea Fleet. The distribution of antipiracy ETF port calls is also split roughly evenly; the North Sea Fleet carried out approximately 29 percent, East Sea Fleet approximately 36 percent, and South Sea Fleet approximately 35 percent.

Third, nearly all ETF port calls either are for replenishment or are friendly visits conducted after the operational part of the antipiracy deployment is complete. Only 6 of 125 total ETF port calls included naval drills along with these two functions. This may be because ETFs returning to China need rest and refit and may not be in suitable condition to carry out combined exercises at the standard of performance demanded by PLA leadership.

Fourth, almost all non-ETF port calls are friendly visits, and a substantial portion of these are carried out by the PLAN training ship *Zhenghe* and *Peace Ark* on HA/DR activities.[119] All of the 49 port calls made by the North Sea Fleet and the 22 made by South Sea Fleet were friendly visits only. Of the 49 North Sea Fleet non-ETF port calls, 21 were made by the training ship *Zhenghe*. Of the 38 East Sea Fleet non-ETF port calls, 27 included drills, all with the *Peace Ark*. The PLAN also conducted one noncombatant evacuation operation in 2015.

The PLAN began conducting HA/DR activities through port calls as part of a concerted effort beginning in 2010. Figure 12 shows this change in non-ETF outbound naval port calls by function. Nearly all of these port calls were carried out as part of the Harmonious Mission series of deployments by the *Peace Ark* from the East Sea Fleet as mentioned above.

The Harmonious Mission deployments represent an effort to practice seafaring skills in a nonthreatening manner. The PLAN has gained valuable operational experience from participation in antipiracy ETFs while also supporting broader Chinese diplomacy by providing public goods. However, as piracy in the Gulf of Aden decreases, the PLAN may find reduced opportunities for military diplomacy. An expansion in HA/DR missions may provide an opportunity for the PLAN to reap the operational and diplomatic benefits of routine, extended deployments in the context of a less threatening nontraditional security operation.

Educational and Functional Exchanges

Overview and Context. PLA education and academic exchanges (院校交流) can be categorized into academic institution leader visits, cadet and professional military education student delegation visits, training foreign military personnel at PLA military educational institutions, and individual PLA officers studying abroad.[120] The PLA also conducts functional exchanges with foreign militaries on specific subjects, including operations, logistics, management, and military medicine. Functional exchanges usually involve visiting expert delegations, and often are conducted by individual PLA services under the direction of the MND/Foreign Affairs Office (now the CMC Office of International Military Cooperation).[121]

Although the PLA has published some aggregate data in its 2000, 2006, and 2008 defense white papers, finding specifics on educational and functional exchanges is difficult. The white papers indicate a steady increase in Chinese military personnel studying abroad, from "more than 200 Chinese military personnel" in Russia, Germany, France, Great Britain, Pakistan, Bangladesh, Thailand, and Kuwait in 1999–2000 to "over 900 military students" studying in more than 30 countries in 2007–2008. The 2008 defense white paper also notes that "twenty military educational institutions in China have established and maintained inter-collegiate exchange relations with their counterparts in over 20 countries, including the United States, Russia, Japan, and Pakistan. Meanwhile, some 4,000 military personnel from more than 130 countries have come to China to study at Chinese military educational institutions." The lack of comparable data makes it difficult to observe any change in trends since the 18th Party Congress. That said, it is clear the PLA has a robust military education and academic exchange program.[122] Some examples are discussed below.

General Staff Department and CMC Academic Institution Exchanges. The PLA's National Defense University (国防大学), which was created in 1985 and is directly subordinate to the CMC, has a robust exchange program with multiple countries.[123] NDU has formal relations with at least seven countries, including the United States, Australia, and South Korea. Each year, NDU hosts about 100 foreign groups and organizes visits abroad to attend international conferences and enhance PLA educational programs. For example, NDU usually hosts a delegation of new flag officers from the U.S. NDU's Capstone Course and sends PLA major generals in its strategic course for a 7- to 10-day trip to one or more foreign countries.

NDU's College of Defense Studies (CDS) is the PLA's primary institution for graduate-level military education for foreign students. Its course offerings include a year-long Defense and Strategic Studies Course, a 5-month Advanced Command Course (in Russian and Spanish), and a 20-day International Symposium Course.[124] In September 2014, CDS awarded its first master's in military science degrees to 61 foreign military students who completed the 2-year program.[125] CDS is located on a separate campus at Changping and is both geographically and organizationally separate from the regular courses NDU offers to PLA officers. As of 2010, CDS had reportedly trained more than 4,000 officers from more than 150 countries.[126]

Two specialized PLA universities, the PLA University of Science and Technology (PLAUST) in Nanjing and the PLA National University of Defense Technology (NUDT) in Changsha, also engage in a range of cooperation with foreign partners, including sponsoring conferences, competitions, and training sessions for foreign experts, military officers, and cadets. For example, PLAUST has held a biennial international cadets' week training program since 2005, with 20 foreign army cadets from 10 countries (Argentina, Brazil, Japan, Mexico, the Netherlands, Thailand, Turkey, United Kingdom, United States, and Uruguay) participating in the 2013 edition along with 16 PLA cadets from PLAUST and the PLA NUDT.[127]

Service Functional and Academic Exchanges. The PLA services each have their own command colleges, technical schools, and military academies to conduct specialized training. (The PLA military education system is expected to undergo a major restructuring and consolidation in 2017.) Many of these institutions conduct a variety of functional and academic exchanges with foreign counterparts. For example, the PLAAF reported in November 2014 that more than 50 foreign air force commanders and chiefs of staff had visited China in the past few years and that it had sent more than 600 senior science and technology officers from units and academic institutions to visit and study abroad.[128] The PLAAF reportedly hosts more than 90 foreign delegations (1,500 personnel) per year.

Although it is difficult to track PLAAF functional exchanges with different countries, the following examples provide snapshots of exchanges with various countries. In December 2014, PLAAF commander General Ma Xiaotian hosted the Portuguese air force chief of staff, where they stated that the two air forces have carried out several pragmatic cooperation activities in personnel training, logistics, and other areas, with great potential for cooperation in other areas.[129] Another example involves PLAAF Command College visits to the United States. In May 2014, Commandant Major General Ma Jian led a 29-member delegation of faculty and students from the college to the United States, where they met with experts at the Center for Naval Analyses and RAND and visited Air University in Montgomery, Alabama, where they met with the university commander and president, Lieutenant General David Fadok, and toured several organizations, including Air War College and the Air Force Research Institute. Like NDU, the PLAAF Command College has established a 2-year master's degree program available in five specialties and three languages (English, French, and Russian). It awarded its first degrees to 20 2-year students from 16 unidentified countries in July 2014.[130] The college has also offered an annual 4-month command course for foreign officers since 2000.

PLA Army and Navy educational institutions offer a similar range of educational programs open to foreign military students, such as a 2013 seminar on information warfare offered by the PLA's Army Command College (南京陆军指挥学院) in Nanjing to army officers from Australia, Canada, Malaysia, Pakistan, Sri Lanka, and the United States.[131] PLA staff colleges offer training to foreign officers in a range of subjects, including flight training, engineering, radar, sonar, telecommunications, artillery, armor, military medicine, foreign languages, and demining.[132] The Rocket Force operates its own command college in Wuhan but is not believed to offer training or have regular interactions with foreign militaries.

In addition to learning from foreign militaries and providing training on technical and military subjects, PLA functional and educational exchanges provide a means of shaping foreign perceptions of China and advancing PRC policy positions in a variety of settings.

Academy of Military Science. The AMS, which is directly subordinate to the CMC, is the PLA's doctrine center and does not appear to train foreign military officers. However, AMS officers interact regularly with foreign military delegations, both in China and in meetings abroad. The AMS president is also president of the China Association for Military Science, which co-sponsors the annual Xiangshan Forum international dialogue.

Nontraditional Security Operations

Overview and Context. China has made a concerted effort to expand military diplomatic activities in the realm of nontraditional security operations, also known as military operations other than war. Such operations support broader Chinese diplomatic and foreign policy goals and provide public goods to the international security environment. Recent examples include Chinese participation in UN peacekeeping operations and international antipiracy escort task forces, the deployment of China's *Peace Ark* hospital ship on overseas humanitarian missions, the deployment of an escort force for Syrian chemical weapons, and the use of PLA assets to search for lost Malaysian Airlines Flight 370 in 2014. In the absence of comparable quantitative data, the qualitative changes and trends in PLA MOOTW activities in recent years are described below.

UN Peacekeeping Operations. The PLA first became involved in United Nations peacekeeping operations (UNPKO) in 1990, when it sent five military observers to the UN Truce Supervision Organization.[133] By the end of September 2014, China had deployed more than

27,000 military personnel around the globe to 23 UN peacekeeping missions.[134] Eighteen PLA soldiers have been killed performing peacekeeping duties. China is the biggest troop and police contributor among the five permanent members of the UN Security Council, and it dispatches the most engineering, transportation, medical support, and security guard troops. China now pays the second largest share of UN peacekeeping costs.[135]

As of January 2017, a total of 2,594 PLA personnel were implementing peacekeeping tasks in nine UN mission areas.[136] The largest Chinese contributions were to the UN Organization Stabilization Mission in the Democratic Republic of the Congo, the African Union/United Nations Hybrid Operation in Darfur, the UN Mission in Liberia, the UN Multidimensional Integrated Stabilization Mission in Mali, the UN Interim Force in Lebanon, and the UN Mission in the Republic of South Sudan, where more than 1,000 PLA soldiers are deployed. Most PLA peacekeeping troops are military observers, engineers, transportation soldiers, and medical officers, but in June 2013 the PLA sent its first security forces as part of its contribution to the mission in Mali.[137] China deployed its first UNPKO infantry battalion abroad to South Sudan in December 2014. The 700-member battalion included 121 officers and 579 enlisted personnel. The battalion was equipped with drones, armored infantry carriers, antitank missiles, mortars, light self-defense weapons, and bulletproof uniforms and helmets, among other weapons that were "completely for self-defense purposes."[138]

The PLA has also continued its active involvement in various peacekeeping training events abroad, training foreign personnel in China, and conducting programs designed to help select qualified personnel from within the Chinese armed forces. For example, in August 2012, China sent observers to Mongolia to observe the 10th Khaan Quest multinational peacekeeping exercise, which involved more than 1,000 soldiers from 10 countries.[139] In June 2014, the PLA hosted a 12-day peacekeeping training session for 33 trainees from 18 countries, including India, Pakistan, Malaysia, South Korea, and other Asian countries.[140] The training took place at the MND's Peacekeeping Training Center, which was created near Beijing in 2009.[141] In September 2014, the center hosted a 3-week course for 40 instructors from 15 countries that included 27 courses and 18 drill subjects.[142] In August 2013, the PLA Institute of International Relations held an examination for 1,670 Chinese field officers seeking positions as UN military observers.[143] They were tested on five subjects, including English and driving. As of 2013, the institute had held 32 training classes for prospective Chinese UN military observers and trained more than 1,300 qualified personnel.

China derives considerable prestige from its contributions of troops, money, and training expertise to UN peacekeeping operations, which comport with its preferred UN-centric model for global governance and support its claim that a stronger PLA is a force for peace. In 2015, President Xi Jinping pledged to commit 8,000 Chinese troops to the UN peacekeeping standby force, making up one-fifth of the 40,000 total troops.[144] UN peacekeeping officials attending the October 2016 Xiangshan Forum in Beijing were given a tour of the Peacekeeping Training Center.[145] China is reportedly seeking to leverage its contributions to UN peacekeeping in order to get a PRC national appointed as Under Secretary General for the UN's Department of Peacekeeping Operations.[146]

Peacekeeping Medical Detachments. Since 2004, the General Logistics Department's health department has overseen the training and dispatching of PLA peacekeeping medical detachments (PMD) from PLA hospitals in the Beijing, Chengdu, Lanzhou, and Nanjing MRs to four African countries—Liberia, Lebanon, Sudan, and Democratic Republic of Congo—on 8-month deployments.[147] Each PMD is assigned to a PLA UNPKO mission and consists of about 50 to 60 male and female doctors and nurses, who are organized into two groups and often overlap with each other in country. While in country, PMDs work in a PLA class-II hospital. In September 2014, the Beijing MR's 302 Hospital, the PLA's only infectious disease hospital, dispatched a PMD to Sierra Leone to deal with the Ebola outbreak. The PMD in Liberia also helped to fight the Ebola outbreak. Of note, in November 2014, China used nine civilian aircraft from China Eastern Airlines and China Cargo Airlines, rather than PLAAF transports, to transport 282 medical staff and 767 tons of medical materials to Guinea, Liberia, and Sierra Leone in support of Ebola rescue efforts.[148]

Antipiracy Escort Task Forces. China's participation in international antipiracy escort task forces is one of the PLA's most visible nontraditional security activities.[149] It began taking part in December 2008, when the PLAN deployed the first of its ETFs to the Gulf of Aden, and it had escorted over 6,000 ships as of November 2016.[150] As of March 2017, the PLAN has deployed 25 ETFs to the Gulf of Aden, each consisting of two destroyers and/or frigates and a comprehensive supply ship, along with associated helicopters, medical personnel, and PLAN special forces personnel.[151]

Peace Ark ***Hospital Ship Deployments.*** China has also deployed the *Peace Ark* on a number of overseas voyages to provide medical care and make port calls to various nations. The *Peace Ark*, commissioned in 2008 and assigned to the East Sea Fleet, has been sent on Harmonious Mission/Peace Mission (和谐使命) HA/DR missions in 2010, 2011, and 2013–2015, as well as other voyages, and has covered more than 70,000 nautical miles.[152] In 2009, the *Peace Ark* traveled down China's coastline providing medical services to local populations and PLA troops stationed on offshore islands. In 2010, in its first overseas deployment, it went to Djibouti, Kenya,

Tanzania, Seychelles, and Bangladesh to provide medical treatment to residents. In late 2011, *Peace Ark* traveled through the Caribbean, visiting Cuba, Jamaica, Trinidad and Tobago, and Costa Rica. In April 2012, it participated in Maritime Cooperation–2012 (海上联合-2012) with Russia, which included a visit to Vladivostok and an HA/DR exercise in Peter the Great Bay in the Sea of Japan. Other recent deployments include Medical Mission–2013 (卫勤使命-2013) to provide post-typhoon Haiyan humanitarian medical aid to the Philippines; Harmonious/Peace Mission–2013, which included a combined disaster relief and military medical science exercise in Brunei under the ASEAN Defense Ministers' Plus mechanism; and deployments to RIMPAC 2014 and Harmonious Mission 2014.[153] The 2015 voyage Harmonious Mission 2015 included stops in seven countries, including Australia, Barbados, French Polynesia, Grenada, Mexico, Peru, and the United States.[154]

Syrian Chemical Weapons Escort Task Force. In accordance with the decision of the Organization for the Prohibition of Chemical Weapons on the removal of Syrian chemical weapons and UN Security Council Resolution 2181 in September 2013, vessels from China, Denmark, Norway, and Russia helped escort the transportation of chemical weapons between December 31, 2013, and June 23, 2014, from Syria to an American vessel for destruction.[155]

During this period, the *Yancheng* guided-missile frigate separated from ETF-16 on December 31, 2013, and headed to the Mediterranean Sea to escort the chemical weapons. On March 8, 2014, the *Huangshan* guided-missile frigate, which had departed by itself from Zhanjiang, Guangdong Province, on February 17, 2014, relieved the *Yancheng*, which returned to its EFT duties. Altogether, the two vessels escorted 20 missions over a 174-day period.

Malaysian Airlines Flight MH370. Immediately following the disappearance of Malaysian Airlines Flight MH370 on March 8, 2014, with 227 passengers onboard, most of whom were Chinese, China began conducting space, airborne, and maritime searches for the aircraft.[156] A total of 26 different countries contributed to the unsuccessful search efforts. Altogether, the PLA assigned 2,273 people and mobilized nine naval vessels, six ship-borne helicopters, and five PLAAF aircraft (including Il-76 and Y-8 transports from the Guangzhou MRAF's 13th Air Division) from March 8 to May 1 to search for the missing plane. Search efforts took place in the Gulf of Thailand, southwest of Sumatra, the South Indian Ocean, and other sea areas, with the PLA conducting air and surface searches, using sonar to search underwater, and employing satellite surveillance.

The aircraft initially operated out of Hainan Island's Sanya Phoenix International Airport before deploying to Malaysia, where they flew out of the Royal Malaysian Air Force base in Subang. They later deployed to Australia, where they flew out of the Royal Australian Air

Force's Pearce Base. The aerial search was called off on April 28. PLAN vessels involved included guided-missile destroyers and frigates, amphibious landing vessels, and comprehensive supply ships, including the three vessels from ETF-17, which participated in search efforts while en route to the Gulf of Aden.

Summary

The trends noted above suggest that the PLA has been steadily increasing the overall amount of military diplomatic activities it carries out with foreign counterparts, with a noticeable increase coinciding roughly with Xi Jinping's ascent to power. This is consistent with Xi's increased emphasis on military diplomacy.[157] Senior-level meetings have fallen since 2010 but continue to make up the overwhelming majority of PLA interactions with foreign militaries. Military exercises, naval port calls, and nontraditional security operations have increased in both visibility and quantity over the past 15 years, while the PLA's functional exchanges with foreign militaries have also likely expanded.

PLA Military Diplomatic Partners

This section examines priorities in Chinese military diplomacy from the country and regional perspective. Which countries does the PLA interact with most? Which countries are the PLA's preferred partners for different types of activities? What priorities does China attach to different regions?

This section addresses these questions using data from various Chinese- and English-language media sources. The PLA Navy conducted its first port call in 1985, and the PLA first began conducting international military exercises in 2002.[158] The data come with two caveats. First, not all senior-level meetings and visits are represented in the dataset due to incomplete information about meetings and visits before 2003. Some meetings and visits certainly occurred before then, but incomplete data make it difficult to assess trends in meetings and visits to specific countries during this period. Second, there is little consistently available quantifiable information that could reveal trends in partners for functional exchanges or military operations other than war. These two categories are therefore not addressed in this quantitatively focused analysis.

The available data reveal three main conclusions. First, PLA military diplomacy focuses heavily on the United States and Russia and on Asian countries on China's periphery. Second, the PLA conducts different types of military activities with different countries. The PLA stresses senior-level contact with Asia and Europe, participates in military exercises with Russia and

SCO nations, and conducts most of its port calls in the Middle East and Asia. Third, the volume of military diplomatic activities with individual countries largely conforms to the priorities implicit in China's chosen labels for relationships with specific countries.

Geographic Focus of PLA Military Diplomacy

PLA military diplomacy appears to place heavy emphasis on great powers, consistent with several strains of Chinese thought on foreign policy and military diplomacy. The United States and Russia are the PLA's two most frequent military diplomatic partners. Both nations participate in a full range of military diplomatic activities with the PLA, including military operations other than war and functional exchanges that are not captured in the quantitative data. Although a senior PLA officer cited interactions with major European militaries as a priority in a 2014 interview, no European country ranks among the PLA's top 10 partners (see table 3).[159]

Beyond the United States and Russia, the pattern of the PLA's military diplomatic interactions over the last 13 years exhibits a clear geographic focus on nations in Asia or near China. Three of the PLA's top 5 partners and 8 of the top 10 are in Asia. Table 4 shows that 41.3 percent of the PLA's military diplomatic interactions from 2003 to 2016 were conducted with countries in Asia, nearly twice as many as Europe, the next most common region.[160]

Figure 13 shows that PLA interactions with Asia and with U.S. treaty allies in Asia have increased significantly since Xi Jinping took power in November 2012. However, increases in

Table 3. The PLA's Top 10 Most Frequent Military Diplomatic Partners, 2003–2016

Overall Rank	Countries	Geographic Region	Military Exercises	Naval Port Calls	Senior-Level Meetings	Grand Total
1	United States	North America	25	9	101	135
2	Russia	Russia	38	4	81	123
3	Pakistan	Asia	29	12	67	108
4	Thailand	Asia	21	9	54	84
5	Australia	Asia	16	8	59	83
6	Vietnam	Asia	2	4	54	60
7	New Zealand	Asia	6	7	43	56
8	Singapore	Asia	10	9	37	56
9	Indonesia	Asia	16	6	33	55
10	India	Asia	18	6	30	54

Table 4. PLA Military Diplomatic Interactions by Geographic Region, 2003–2016

Geographic Region	Military Exercises	Naval Port Calls	Senior-Level Meetings	Grand Total	% of Total Interactions
Asia	204	105	842	1151	41.3
Europe	51	33	543	627	22.5
Africa	13	22	259	294	10.6
South America	8	12	201	221	7.9
Middle East	10	76	113	199	7.2
North America	27	13	130	170	6.1
Russia	38	4	81	123	4.4

overall military diplomatic interactions rose at an even faster pace than interactions with Asian nations, and interactions with Asian nations rose faster than interactions with U.S. allies in Asia. Figure 14 illustrates PLA military relations with U.S. treaty allies in Asia in more detail, showing an increase in these activities beginning in 2012 led by more interactions with Australia and

Figure 13. PLA Military Diplomatic Interactions, 2003–2016

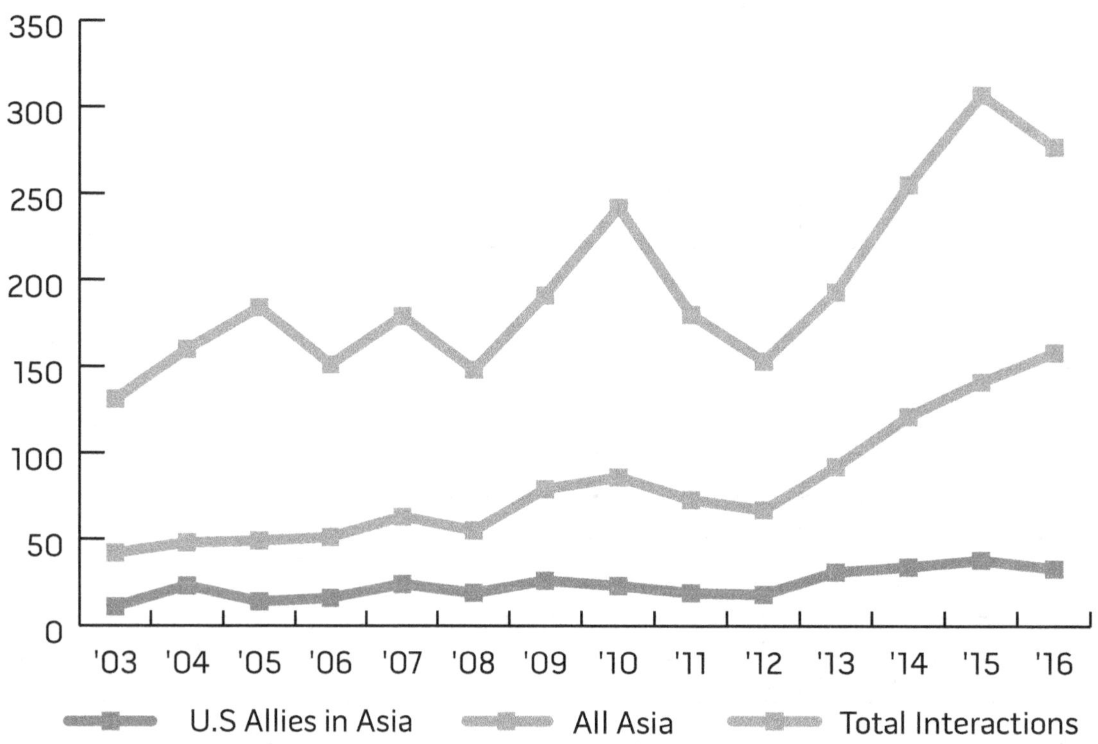

Figure 14. PLA Diplomatic Interactions with U.S. Allies in Asia, 2003–2016

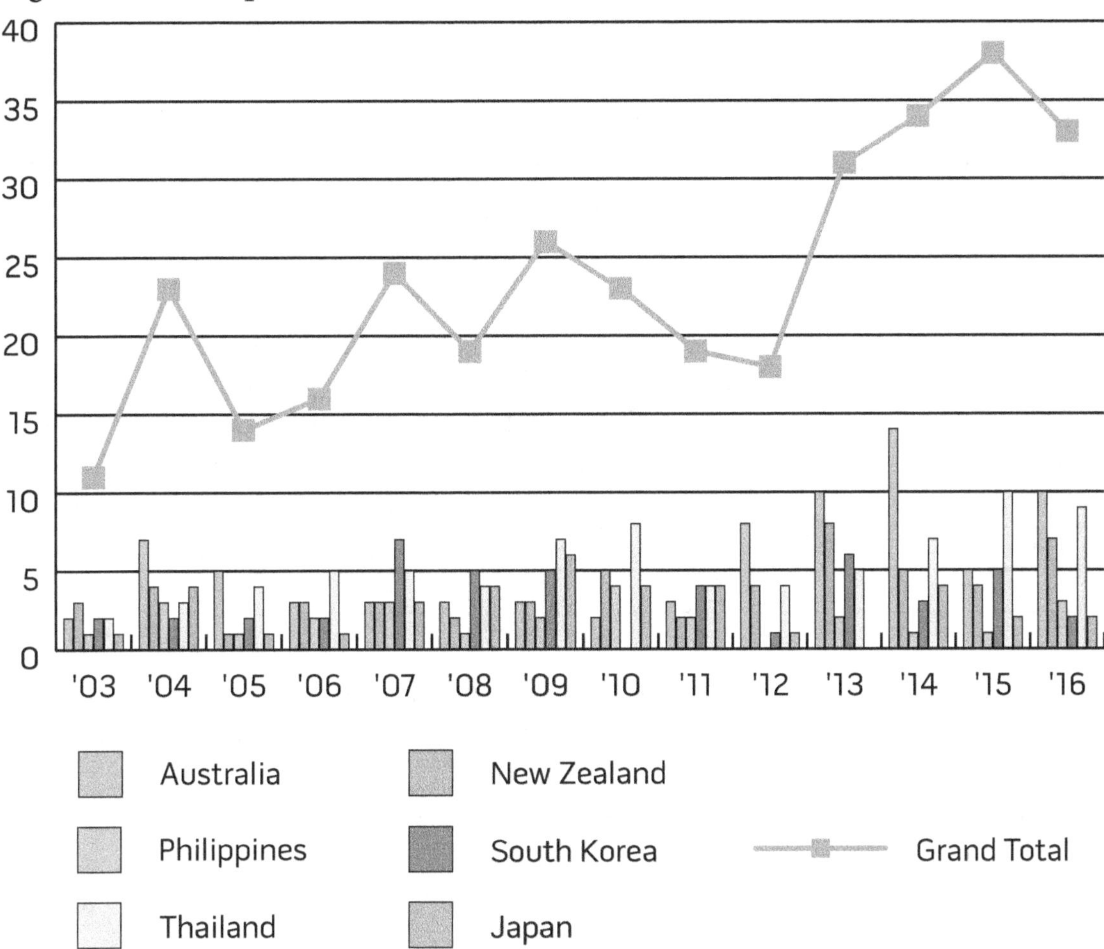

Thailand. Of note, PLA military interactions with U.S. allies Japan and the Philippines declined significantly beginning in 2012 as confrontations with China over maritime territorial disputes (in the East China Sea and South China Sea, respectively) intensified. The Chinese government sought to increase diplomatic pressure on both governments, and the PLA played its part by curtailing interactions with the Japanese and Philippine militaries. A similar reduction in PLA contacts with the South Korean military occurred in 2016 and 2017 as China sought to pressure the government in Seoul not to deploy the Terminal High-Altitude Area Defense (THAAD) missile defense system.[161]

Increased PLA military diplomatic activity in Asia may be a response to the U.S. rebalance to Asia, which was announced in fall 2011 and emphasized an increased U.S. focus on Southeast Asia, or it may reflect guidance from Xi Jinping to increase military diplomacy more generally.

Most of the PLA's military diplomatic activity in Asia involves South and Southeast Asian countries. According to table 5, approximately 54 percent of the PLA's military diplomatic interactions with Asian countries are with 18 countries in Southeast Asia, and interactions with 6 South Asian countries account for some 21 percent of the total activity with Asia.[162] Taken together, these two subregions account for more than 75 percent of the PLA's military interactions with countries in Asia. Figure 15 documents the PLA's military relations in Asia over time, demonstrating that the rate of increase was sharpest for Southeast Asia from 2013 to 2016.

Table 5. PLA Military Diplomatic Interactions in Asia, 2003–2016

	Military Exercises	Naval Port Calls	Senior-Level Meetings	Grand Total	% of Interactions in Asia
Southeast Asia	91	68	466	625	54.30
South Asia	58	33	160	251	21.81
Central Asia	39	0	102	141	12.25
Northeast Asia	16	4	114	134	11.64

Figure 15. Aggregate PLA Military Diplomatic Interactions in Asia, 2003–2016

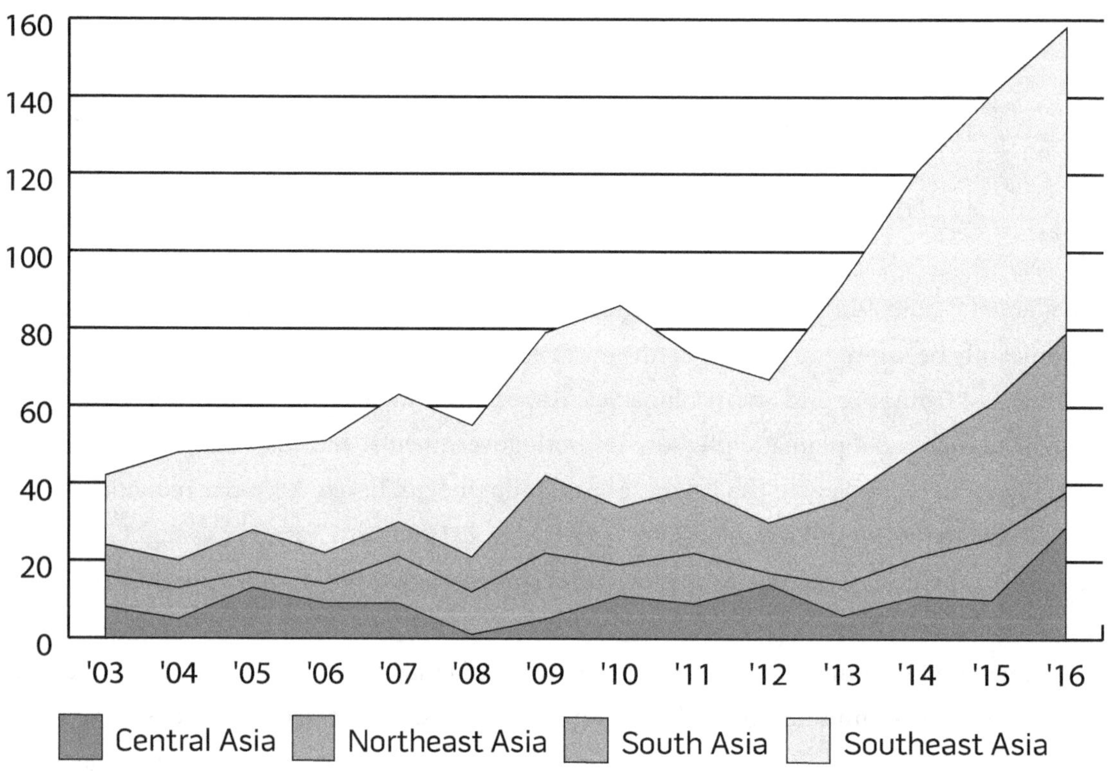

PLA Military Diplomatic Preferences in Detail

The PLA interacts with different foreign partners in different ways. Patterns in these interactions suggest differing levels of cooperation, trust, expediency, and effort between the PLA and specific foreign military diplomatic partners.

The PLA appears to place a strong emphasis on senior-level contact with Europe and countries in Asia, especially in the subregions of Southeast and South Asia. Contacts with militaries in Asia were detailed in the previous section. PLA officers also visit Europe frequently. Nearly 27 percent of total senior-level meetings held abroad take place in Europe, and 24 percent of the attendees at meetings hosted in China are from European countries. Belarus leads European countries in hosting meetings with visiting Chinese officers, followed by Italy, Germany, Romania, and the United Kingdom. Figures 16 and 17 highlight the PLA's emphasis on senior-level engagement with Asia-Pacific and European countries.

Figure 16. Senior-Level Visits Abroad by Geographic Region, 2003–2016

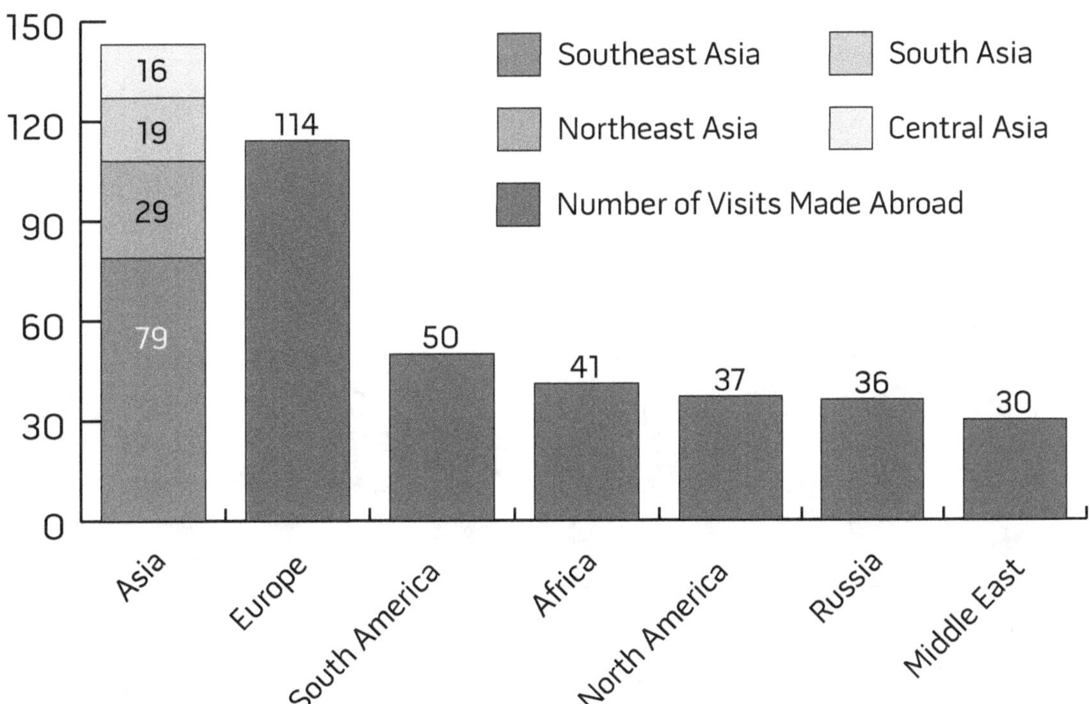

Figure 17. Senior-Level Meetings Abroad and Hosted in China by Region, 2003–2016

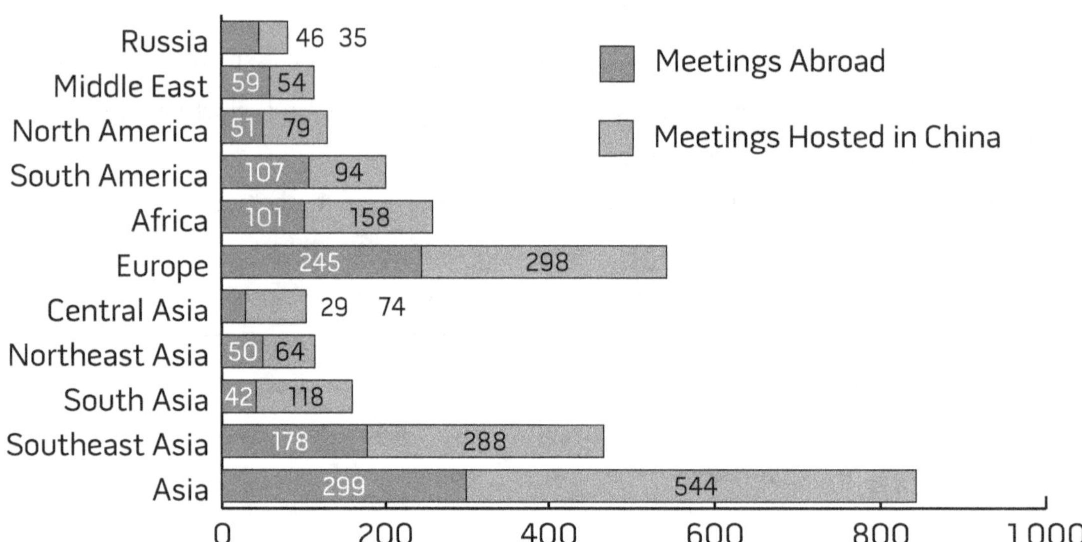

Figure 18. Number of PLA Visits Abroad, 2003–2016

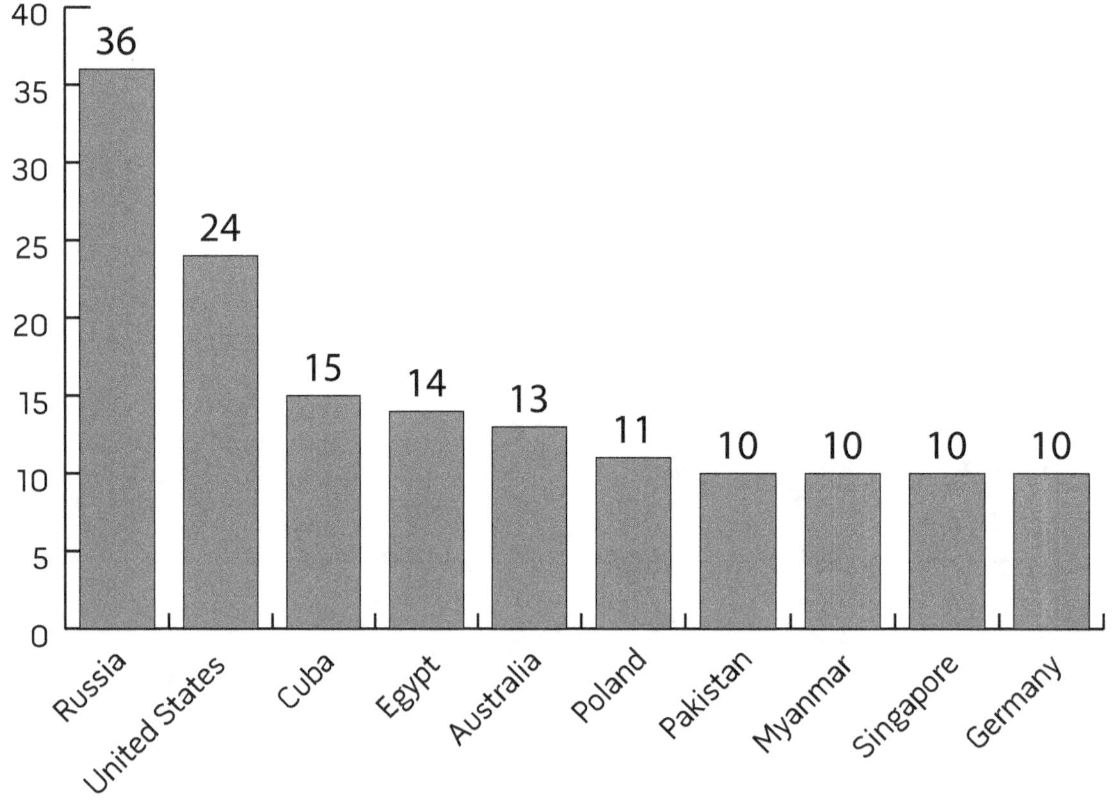

Figure 18 shows the most frequent destinations for PLA senior-level visits abroad from 2003 to 2016; during this period, the PLA dispatched the most delegations to Russia, the United States, and Cuba.

The differential between senior-level visits sent and those hosted by the PLA can indicate which country is departing from the diplomatic protocol of reciprocity and trying harder to build the bilateral relationship. Countries meeting with the PLA in China more frequently than the PLA visits their respective countries are putting more effort into their military diplomatic engagement with China and have large positive differentials in senior-level meetings.[163] Figure 19 shows that the United States, Pakistan, and Australia have visited the PLA in China more often than PLA officers have visited their respective countries. Conversely, the PLA places more

Figure 19. Largest Differentials Between Meetings Hosted in China and Abroad

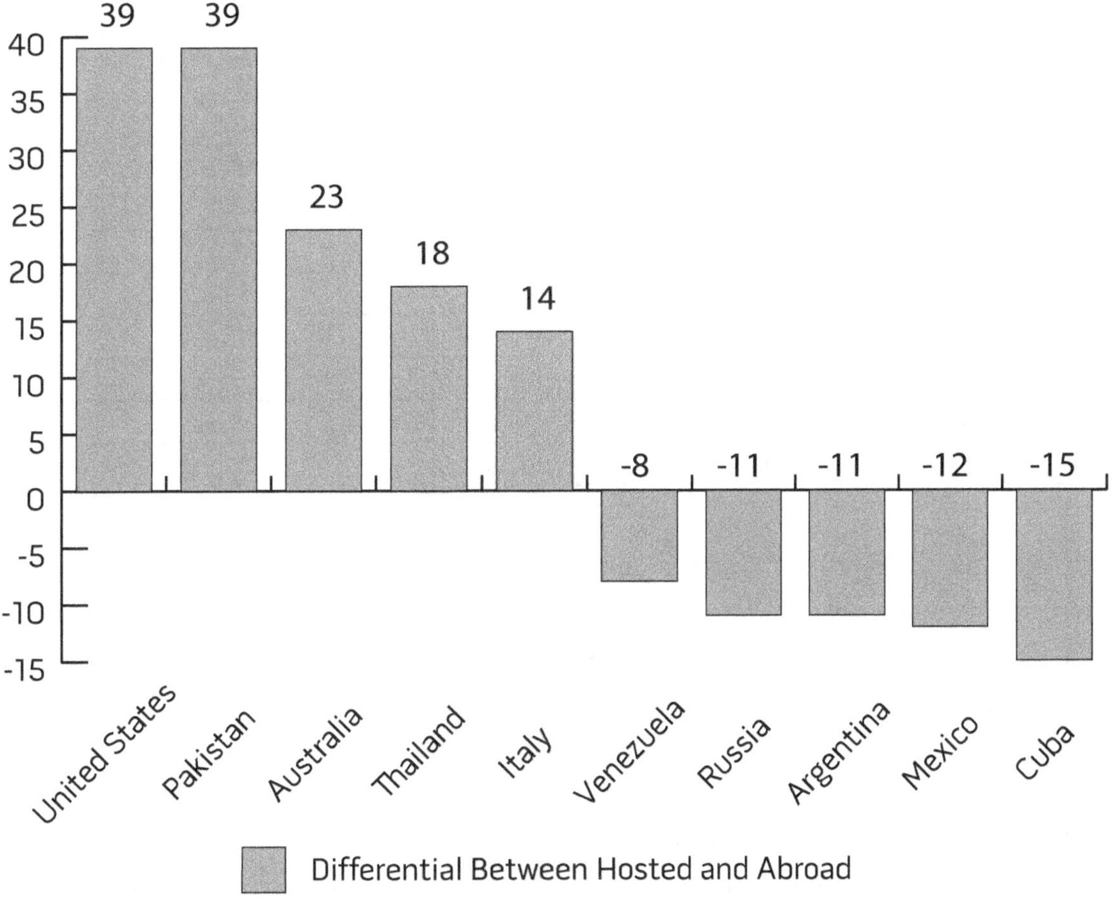

emphasis on senior-level engagement with Cuba, Mexico, Argentina, and Russia than those militaries place on China. As already noted, there has been a drop in the volume of PLA senior visits overseas since 2012, and more countries have become willing to send senior military and defense officials to visit China without reciprocal visits from their Chinese counterparts.

Although the PLA stresses senior-level contact with Europe and Asia, broadly speaking, the PLA's most frequent international partners for military exercises are Russia and SCO nations. Russia, Pakistan, and the United States have the most military exercise interactions with the PLA, while Kazakhstan, Kyrgyzstan, and India have the largest proportion of military exercise interactions. The PLA's most frequent partners for combat drills, the most complex and sensitive types of military exercises, are Russia, Pakistan, and Kyrgyzstan. Table 6 shows the PLA's most frequent partners for military exercises and for combat exercises.

Table 6. Top PLA Partners for Military Exercises, 2003–2016

Number of Military Exercise Interactions (Number of Combat Exercises)		Military Exercise Interactions as % of Total Military Diplomatic Interactions	
Russia	38 (19)	Kazakhstan	38.1
Pakistan	29 (7)	Kyrgyzstan	34.5
United States	25 (0)	India	33.0
Thailand	21 (5)	Armenia	33.0
India	18 (0)	Tajikistan	32.4
Kazakhstan	16 (6)	Russia	30.9
Indonesia	16 (3)	France	30.2
Australia	16 (0)	Indonesia	29.1
France	13 (0)	Nigeria	28.6
Tajikistan	11 (6)	Venezuela	27.3

The demanding characteristics of military exercises suggest a higher degree of coordination and interoperability between the PLA and its most prolific partners for military exercises and likely reflect the PLA's effort to learn tactics, techniques, and procedures from Russia and SCO partners. Military exercises are the most complex and sensitive military diplomatic activities the PLA can conduct with foreign partners, and combat exercises require high levels of confidence, coordination, and planning to execute. Some countries such as the United States, India, France, and Australia regularly exercise with the PLA but are reluctant to conduct combat exercises due to political constraints on military relations with China and reluctance to help the

PLA build its combat capabilities. The only truly "joint" international military exercise the PLA participates in is the Peace Mission series of drills with Russia and other SCO partners.

While patterns in its international military exercises suggest that the PLA is learning from the drills, its most frequent destinations for naval port calls are either driven by operational demands or are part of a carefully tailored effort to reassure China's immediate neighbors about the benign nature of its naval buildup and its intentions writ large. The overwhelming proportion of the port calls made by China's antipiracy escort task forces occur in Middle Eastern nations as replenishment visits for ETF ships, while the most frequent non-ETF port call destinations are nations in the Asia-Pacific region. Table 7 shows the PLAN's most frequent port call destinations. The PLA's establishment of a logistics support facility in Djibouti in 2016 is likely to reduce the volume of ETF replenishment visits to other foreign ports in the future.

The PLA's non-ETF port calls are mostly in the Asia-Pacific region and reflect a gradual expansion of the PLA's naval reach. The most frequent destinations for non-ETF port calls were New Zealand, the United States, Australia, and the South Asian countries of Pakistan and India. All of the non-ETF visits in the top 10 PLAN port call destinations were friendly port calls or HA/DR missions from the *Peace Ark* designed to generate favorable publicity for the PLAN. The use of friendly visits (and the absence of naval drills) likely reflects an effort by China to reassure its neighbors about the benign nature of its naval buildup, even as PLAN ships begin to venture farther into the South Pacific, Western Pacific, and Indian oceans.

The PLA carries out different military diplomatic activities with different partners. The data from 2003 to 2016 indicate that the PLA strongly emphasizes senior-level meetings with

Table 7. Most Frequent PLAN Port Call Destinations, 2003–2016

Overall Port Calls		ETF Port Calls		Non-ETF Port Calls	
Oman	25	Oman	25	New Zealand	7
Djibouti	23	Djibouti	22	United States	7
Pakistan	12	Yemen	10	Australia	6
Yemen	11	Saudi Arabia	7	Pakistan	5
Sri Lanka	9	Sri Lanka	7	India	5
Singapore	9	Pakistan	7	Thailand	5
Thailand	9	Singapore	6	Bangladesh	5
United States	9	Thailand	4	Indonesia	4
Australia	8	Malaysia	3	Philippines	4
Saudi Arabia	7	Greece	3	Russia	3

counterparts in Asia, Europe, the United States, and Russia; participates in the most military exercises with Russia and SCO countries; and conducts the most port calls in the Middle East and the Asia-Pacific region. These trends suggest that the PLA seeks to improve military relations with European and Asian nations, while the United States, Pakistan, and Australia are working to improve relations with the PLA. The PLA appears most comfortable participating in complex military exercises with Russia and SCO nations, suggesting a higher level of trust and cooperation between the PLA and these militaries. Most PLA port calls in the Middle East are intended to meet operational requirements of PLAN counterpiracy missions, while PLA port calls in the Asia-Pacific are mostly friendly port calls rather than exercises.

The Broader Strategic Context of PLA Military Diplomacy

PLA military diplomatic activities are ostensibly subordinate to the broader contours of Chinese diplomacy and foreign affairs directives, and trends in PLA military diplomacy should therefore reflect China's overall strategic orientation.[164] How well do PLA military relations conform to the broader strategic priorities that China assigns to various nations around the world?

China began establishing strategic partnerships (战略伙伴关系) with various countries in the early to mid-1990s under Jiang Zemin, and the number and types of partnerships increased under Hu Jintao. Although several partner countries have worked out unique names for their bilateral relationships with China, the Chinese foreign ministry generally employs specific terms to distinguish between higher and lower priority relationships. The first distinction is between countries that are *partners* (伙伴) and those with which China only has *relationships* (关系) or no specific relationship label. The second distinction is between partnerships that are *strategic* (战略) and those that are merely *friendly* (友好). The third distinction is between *comprehensive* (全面) and *cooperative* (合作) relationships, with comprehensive describing a broader range of cooperation. Within this hierarchy, a comprehensive strategic partnership (全面战略伙伴关系) is toward the top of the scale, while a friendly cooperative relationship (友好合作关系) denotes a less important relationship.[165] The United States and Japan are important exceptions to this pattern. China sought a strategic partnership with the United States but ultimately settled for calling the bilateral relationship a "new type of major country relationship." Nevertheless, Chinese diplomats consider the U.S.-China relationship as equivalent to a strategic partnership. Japan is a second anomaly, since historical animosities made China reluctant to accord Japan "strategic" status or endorse a full partnership. Accordingly, the two countries are called "mutually cooperative partners," even though Japan receives much more diplomatic attention from China than that term suggests.

While Chinese scholars emphasize that China's strategic partnerships are broader relationships and not military alliances, there are at least two reasons that military diplomacy might be correlated to the relationship labels that Beijing uses.[166] First, because military diplomacy is subordinate to higher level foreign policy guidance, the volume and types of military diplomatic activities should correspond to those countries with higher overall strategic priority. Second, the comparatively greater amount of effort required to carry out foreign military relations and the higher sensitivity of military relations suggest that those ties would be easier to maintain with countries that China prioritizes. Given the strong top-down nature and complexity of Chinese military diplomacy, observers would expect that higher strategic priority should translate into more military diplomatic interactions.

Preliminary empirical evidence indicates that this intuitive observation is broadly true. Despite a wide variety of labels, certain terms appear to be correlated with higher levels of PLA military diplomatic interaction. To determine if certain terms were likely to lead to higher levels of PLA military diplomatic activity, we used multivariate regression analysis with the amount of military diplomatic interaction as the dependent variable, and the eight terms used with multiple countries as independent variables: *strategic, comprehensive/all-round/all-weather, cooperative, friendly, relationship, partnership/partner, new type,* and *no specific relationship.* These independent variables were coded as dummy variables—that is, if a country's relationship label contained a given term, it was assigned a value of one; otherwise, they were coded with zeros. Comprehensive, all-round, and all-weather were coded together as one variable because these terms were believed to mean the same thing; partnership and partner were similarly coded together. The United States was coded as a strategic partner because Chinese diplomats consider the U.S.-China relationship equivalent to a strategic partnership, even though strategic is not included in the label.

The regression analysis in table 8 shows that strategic was associated with the biggest increase in military diplomatic activity, followed by comprehensive/all-round/all-weather and cooperative. The increases in military diplomatic interactions caused by these three variables are represented by positive coefficients and were statistically significant, with p-values below 0.05. The term new type also caused a statistically significant increase in military diplomatic activity, but the increase is skewed upward because the moniker applies only to the United States and Finland. Other variables were associated with both increases and decreases in military diplomatic activity, but these results were not statistically significant enough (at the 0.05 level) to rule out change attributable to random chance. China uses many of these terms liberally and interchangeably among different countries.

Table 8. Regression Analysis on Key Terms Used in PRC Strategic Partnerships and Relationships

Regression Statistics					
Multiple R	0.612684742				
R Square	0.375382593				
Adjusted R Square	0.340438962				
Standard Error	18.1142473				
Observations	152				
ANOVA					
	Df	*SS*	*MS*	*F*	*Significance F*
Regression	8	28199.19235	3524.899	10.74252	9.1342E-12
Residual	143	46922.0116	328.126		
Total	151	75121.20395			

	Coefficients	*Std. Error*	*t Stat*	*P-value*	*Lower 95%*	*Upper 95%*
Intercept	8.5000	12.8087	0.6636	0.508008	-16.8189	33.8189
Strategic	**31.9997**	7.0851	4.5165	**1.31E-05**	17.9946	46.0048
Comprehensive/All-Round/All-Weather	**14.3316**	4.2033	3.4096	**0.000846**	6.0229	22.6403
Cooperative	**13.5965**	5.4097	2.5134	**0.013068**	2.9032	24.2899
Friendly	9.8876	7.0703	1.3985	0.164136	-4.0882	23.8634
Relationship	-21.4982	16.6754	-1.2892	0.199404	-54.4603	11.4639
Partnership/Partner	-24.3482	15.1674	-1.6053	0.110634	-54.3296	5.6331
New Type	**73.6251**	13.9041	5.2952	**4.39E-07**	46.1409	101.1093
No Specific Relationship	0.2368	13.1415	0.0180	0.985646	-25.7398	26.2135

While the regression analysis suggests that strategic, comprehensive, and cooperative are associated with the greatest increases in military diplomatic activity, the results should not be over-interpreted. The analysis only tested for the independent impact of single terms on the amount of military diplomatic activity; it did not test for the interaction between these terms—that is, what the impact would have been if strategic and comprehensive occurred simultaneously. Additionally, the R-Square value of 0.375 suggests that the regression line may not be the best fit for the data.

In some cases, the data do not reflect the known historical evolution of the terms. For instance, while partnership is associated with a decrease in military diplomatic activity, this change is not statistically significant, likely due to the increasing and widespread use of partnership over time, which dilutes the hierarchical importance of the term. Past analysis has indicated that partnership was mostly reserved for major powers in the 1990s, was broadened to include major regional powers in the 2000s, and was subsequently applied as a catch-all term to any country with a good relationship with China.[167] Several countries were "upgraded" from relationship to partnership as relations with China developed, suggesting that the Chinese emphasize partnerships over relationships.[168] The regression does not account for this upgrading and the hierarchical priority that the Chinese ascribe to partnerships.

The hierarchy of strategic partnerships and the empirical analysis also do not account for China's caution in military diplomacy with countries that are under UN sanctions or where close strategic ties might cause serious tensions with the United States. For instance, North Korea is China's one treaty ally and depends heavily on China for economic aid and political support. Yet the countries do not have a strategic partnership and have only limited military diplomatic contacts: North Korea ranks 45th in overall PLA interactions, with no military exercise interactions, 1 naval port call, and 21 senior-level meetings since Hu Jintao took power in 2003. Similarly, China's arms sales and security ties with Iran have long been a source of tension in Sino-U.S. relations due to U.S. concerns about Iran's support for terrorism and pursuit of nuclear weapons. China did not establish a strategic partnership with Iran until UN sanctions were removed after Iran signed an agreement restricting its nuclear program.[169] PLA interactions with the Iranian military were also limited, with Iran ranking 56th in overall PLA interactions, hosting only 1 naval port call and 11 senior meetings from 2003 to 2016. Once sanctions were lifted and China established a strategic partnership with Iran, Chinese and Iranian military forces participated in four separate military competitions (exercises) in August 2016.

The overall volume of PLA military diplomatic activities with different partners indicates that the PLA's military relations generally correspond with the broader strategic priorities laid out by China's higher level leadership. In particular, the PLA's military relations appear to reflect the priorities expressed in China's convoluted partnership classification system.

Conclusion and Implications

The analysis in this study reveals a concerted PLA effort to use military relations to achieve a variety of objectives, with a particular emphasis on supporting overall Chinese diplomacy, learning new skills and benchmarking the PLA against foreign militaries, and shaping the security environment. Other military diplomatic objectives such as intelligence gathering and building partner capacity appear to be lower priority objectives.

Almost all military diplomatic activities support China's overall diplomatic efforts in some fashion. The country and regional priorities in China's military diplomatic interactions appear to correspond closely with the priorities in China's wider foreign policy. This includes a broad focus on building good strategic relations with major powers such as the United States and Russia and the priority placed on countries in Asia and along China's periphery. Moreover, the volume of military relations also appears to correspond with the naming taxonomy used to indicate priorities in China's relations with various foreign countries.

The PLA's growing participation in nontraditional security operations, military exercises, and functional exchanges highlights PLA efforts to learn new skills and benchmark the capabilities of its forces against those of other nations. PLA participation in military competitions is an explicit form of benchmarking and reflects greater confidence that PLA units will not embarrass themselves. The PLA's expanded program of exercises and functional exchanges also provides opportunities to learn from foreign militaries.

Analysis of the PLA's military relations from 2003 to 2016 confirms that the PLA is using military diplomacy to shape China's security environment. For instance, the majority of non-ETF port calls are friendly port visits that occur in Asia, highlighting Chinese attempts to assuage neighbors concerned about its new naval might. The *Peace Ark* routinely stops at multiple Asian ports in order to cultivate China's image as a benign power that can make positive contributions to regional security. Since 2010, however, shaping efforts have increasingly displayed military capabilities rather than downplaying them. Military exercises in particular have become more combat-oriented and sometimes appear designed to deter or discourage potential opponents using specific capabilities. For example, China partnered with Russia to carry out a missile defense exercise in May 2016, shortly after a row over U.S. deployment of the THAAD missile defense system in South Korea.[170] The two countries also highlighted their missile defense cooperation and opposition to U.S. missile defense deployments in a joint press conference at the Xiangshan Forum in October 2016.

While the PLA's foreign military relations have placed strong emphasis on supporting China's overall diplomatic posture, learning new skills and benchmarking, and shaping the security environment, the PLA has apparently placed less emphasis on active intelligence-gathering and building partner capacity. Almost all PLA military diplomatic interactions present opportunities to collect intelligence, and the PLA takes full advantage of those opportunities. However, few military diplomatic activities appear to have intelligence collection as their primary focus.

Every contact with a foreign military is an opportunity to gain knowledge, but activities involving deeper operational contacts are likely to have more intelligence value. For instance, PLAN exercises with the Russian navy provide hands-on opportunities to learn from Russia and to accurately assess the technical capabilities of Russian weapons systems and the operational proficiency of Russian crews.

Unlike the United States, building partner military capacity does not appear to be an especially important goal of PLA military diplomacy. Although some military diplomatic interactions help build partner capacity, the PLA's foreign military relations do not emphasize this objective. Military diplomatic activities are typically framed as efforts to improve ties with foreign militaries.[171] Building the capacity of foreign military partners appears to be a means of strengthening relations rather than an end in itself. China does conduct activities intended to improve the military and domestic security capabilities of some foreign partners, but these do not necessarily fall within the scope of military diplomacy. For instance, Chinese arms sales are conducted by state-owned arms manufacturers, internal security assistance falls under the purview of the Ministry of State Security and the Ministry of Public Security, and advice on censorship or control of the Internet would be the province of the Cyberspace Administration of China and other organizations.[172]

The PLA is using its program of foreign military relations to pursue a range of objectives, but the increased volume of military diplomatic activities documented in this study does not necessarily translate into success. The PLA's foreign military relations are subject to a number of international and domestic constraints. First and foremost, PLA military diplomacy is constrained by what activities foreign counterparts are willing and able to do with the PLA. China's increasingly assertive behavior on the international stage could reduce the efficacy of its military diplomatic efforts and reduce its neighbors' willingness to interact with the PLA; China will find it harder to reassure its neighbors if it is also bullying them. Resource limitations, including the small staff of the CMC Office of International Military Cooperation and the demands placed on senior PLA officers by ongoing military reforms, are likely to reduce the number of PLA military engagements in 2017 and perhaps for the next several years.

Other constraints stem from the nature of the Chinese system and the desire of the CCP to exert tight control over the military. Chinese culture emphasizes form over substance, and China's strategic culture makes it averse to binding security agreements. PLA officers are subject to top-down directives, tight control of political messaging, and the need to protect information about PLA capabilities, which inhibits candid conversations with foreign counterparts.[173] Most PLA interlocutors are not empowered to negotiate or share their real views, which makes it difficult to build strong personal or institutional ties with foreign counterparts.[174] As a result, much of China's military diplomatic activity consists of formal exchanges of scripted talking points during senior-level meetings, occasional naval port calls, and simple scripted military exercises focused on nontraditional security issues. These activities support existing relationships but are unlikely to build much strategic trust or support deeper military cooperation.

The PLA's program of military diplomacy is best understood as a product of these constraints. Many of the trends observed in this paper are reflections of long-standing, higher level Chinese diplomatic strategy, consistent with military diplomacy's hierarchical position in China's top-down system of governance. Some of the trends noted here will not be surprising to close observers of the PLA; for instance, closer Sino-Russian defense ties and China's cultivation of influence on Australia and Thailand have been years in the making. The PLA's role in these military diplomatic trends appears to be a slower-moving manifestation of broader Chinese strategy.

This does not mean the PLA's military diplomacy is insignificant or does not warrant analytic and policy attention. The PLA's growing involvement in a web of bilateral and multilateral foreign military relationships produces pressure for greater transparency and for adherence to international rules and norms. For example, after blocking agreement on the Code for Unplanned Encounters at Sea (CUES) in the Western Pacific Naval Symposium for several years, the PLAN eventually accepted the agreement while hosting the symposium in Qingdao in 2014 and has subsequently employed CUES in interactions with foreign navies. Military-to-military relationships have also been useful for establishing military hotlines and rules governing air and maritime encounters that can reduce the risk of crisis or conflict.[175] However, PLA scholars believe military diplomacy can also be used to escalate crises when beneficial to national interests (for example, by cutting off planned military exercises or exchanges), making military diplomatic activities a bargaining chip that Beijing can wield.[176] The PLA can be expected to use military diplomacy to try to win support for China's diplomatic objectives, such as China's cooperation with Russia to oppose U.S. missile defense deployments and to promote an international code of conduct for space weapons.[177] In some cases, these efforts may erode or modify existing international norms in ways that work against U.S. interests.

U.S. policymakers should also focus on the PLA's ability to use military diplomacy to improve its operational capabilities or build strategic relationships that give it access to strategic airfields and ports. U.S. allies and partners with advanced military capabilities should be discouraged from helping the PLA learn to conduct advanced combat operations or sharing details about U.S. military capabilities and tactics. At the same time, U.S. allies and partners will want to interact with the PLA as part of their efforts to manage their relations with China, and U.S. policymakers should not try to stop them. PLA military diplomatic activities might also advance Chinese national interests at the expense of U.S. interests. For example, Chinese transfers of advanced military capabilities to potential U.S. adversaries such as Iran and North Korea or countries providing PLA significant access to bases, airfields, or ports in strategically important areas should be of concern to U.S. policymakers. Military diplomatic interactions with any of these characteristics would likely be the result of national-level strategic decisionmaking, not lower level PLA decisions.

While these developments should concern U.S. policymakers, not all potentially alarming trends in PLA military diplomacy are as easily noticed. Functional and academic exchanges that improve the PLA's warfighting capability are difficult to measure or detect until well after they have occurred. The most worrisome developments may be ones we cannot observe or measure quantitatively.

The patterns observed in the PLA's military relations from 2003 to 2016 indicate that although PLA military diplomatic activity has increased in volume and expanded in scope, this increased activity has not necessarily translated into increased Chinese influence. In many cases, the volume and type of activity may be an indicator of the quality of China's diplomatic relations and security cooperation with a particular country rather than an effective means of expanding Chinese influence. The data in this study indicate that the PLA has continued to expand its foreign military relations program in accordance with directives from the highest levels of China's leadership. This means that shifts in functional and regional emphasis in the PLA's foreign military relations likely reflect China's broader national priorities as well as shifts in PLA capabilities and interests.

Appendix. PLA Military Diplomatic Interactions, 2003–2016

Country	Military Exercises	Naval Port Calls	Senior-Level Meetings	Grand Total
United States	25	9	101	135
Russia	38	4	81	123
Pakistan	29	12	67	108
Thailand	21	9	54	84
Australia	16	8	59	83
Vietnam	2	4	54	60
New Zealand	6	7	43	56
Singapore	10	9	37	56
Indonesia	16	6	33	55
India	18	6	30	54
Malaysia	10	6	35	51
South Korea	4	3	42	49
Belarus	9		40	49
France	13	4	26	43
Germany	4	3	35	42
Kazakhstan	16		26	42
Italy	2	3	36	41
United Kingdom	7	2	31	40
Bangladesh	4	6	29	39
Myanmar	1	4	34	39
Japan	6		33	39
Egypt	3	3	32	38
Chile		1	36	37
Romania	2	1	34	37
Brazil	3	3	29	35
Cuba		2	33	35
Laos	1		34	35
Tajikistan	11		23	34
Cambodia	2	3	28	33
South Africa	2	5	25	32
Djibouti		23	8	31
Sri Lanka	3	9	18	30

Appendix. PLA Military Diplomatic Interactions, 2003–2016, cont.

Country	Military Exercises	Naval Port Calls	Senior-Level Meetings	Grand Total
Greece	2	4	24	30
Finland		1	28	29
Oman	1	25	3	29
Poland		1	28	29
Kyrgyzstan	10		19	29
Philippines	3	5	20	28
Tanzania	1	2	24	27
Turkey	3	3	20	26
Bulgaria		1	25	26
Hungary	1		24	25
Mongolia	6		18	24
Argentina		1	21	22
North Korea		1	21	22
Switzerland			21	21
Nepal	4		15	19
Brunei	3	1	14	18
Mexico		2	16	18
Serbia	1		16	17
Sweden		1	16	17
Canada	2	2	13	17
Uzbekistan	2		14	16
Namibia	1	1	14	16
Iran	4	1	11	16
Saudi Arabia	2	7	7	16
Sudan		1	14	15
Afghanistan			15	15
Zambia			14	14
Zimbabwe	2		12	14
Yemen		11	3	14
Ecuador		2	12	14
Ukraine		2	11	13
Mozambique		1	12	13

Appendix. PLA Military Diplomatic Interactions, 2003–2016, cont.

Country	Military Exercises	Naval Port Calls	Senior-Level Meetings	Grand Total
Portugal		3	10	13
Peru		2	11	13
Angola	2	1	10	13
Jordan		1	11	12
Kenya		2	10	12
Bolivia			12	12
Israel		1	10	11
Venezuela	3		8	11
Denmark	2	1	8	11
Croatia		1	10	11
Tunisia		1	9	10
Slovakia			10	10
Uruguay			10	10
Colombia	2		8	10
Spain			10	10
Norway			9	9
Czech Republic	1		7	8
Netherlands		1	7	8
Algeria		2	6	8
Maldives		1	7	8
Uganda			8	8
Syria			8	8
Ethiopia			8	8
Macedonia			8	8
Nigeria	2	1	4	7
Austria			7	7
Gabon	1		6	7
Morocco		1	6	7
United Arab Emirates		2	4	6
Togo			6	6
Lebanon			6	6
Cameroon	1	1	4	6

Appendix. PLA Military Diplomatic Interactions, 2003–2016, cont.

Country	Military Exercises	Naval Port Calls	Senior-Level Meetings	Grand Total
Seychelles		3	3	6
Belgium			6	6
Ghana	1		5	6
Congo			6	6
Papua New Guinea		1	5	6
Armenia	2		4	6
Qatar		1	5	6
Turkmenistan			5	5
Fiji		2	3	5
Guyana			5	5
DR Congo			5	5
Trinidad and Tobago		1	4	5
Suriname			5	5
Botswana			4	4
Mali			4	4
Cyprus			4	4
Tonga		1	3	4
Bosnia-Herzegovina			4	4
Kuwait		1	3	4
Rwanda			3	3
Malta		1	2	3
Liberia			3	3
Senegal		1	2	3
Azerbaijan			3	3
East Timor		1	2	3
Vanuatu		1	2	3
Bahrain		1	2	3
Malawi			3	3
Latvia			3	3
Jamaica		1	2	3

Appendix. PLA Military Diplomatic Interactions, 2003–2016, cont.

Country	Military Exercises	Naval Port Calls	Senior-Level Meetings	Grand Total
Ivory Coast		1	2	3
Barbados		1	2	3
Lesotho			3	3
Grenada		1	1	2
Niger			2	2
Mauritania			2	2
Guinea			2	2
Comoros			2	2
Moldova			2	2
Central African Republic			2	2
Guinea-Bissau			2	2
Lithuania			2	2
Montenegro			2	2
Burundi			2	2
Benin			2	2
Costa Rica		1	1	2
Eritrea			2	2
Cape Verde			2	2
Sierra Leone			2	2
Chad			1	1
Slovenia			1	1
Antigua and Barbuda			1	1
Madagascar			1	1
Mauritius		1		1
Albania			1	1
Estonia			1	1
Grand Total	**349**	**274**	**2,162**	**2,785**

Notes

[1] These dates begin with the first full year of the Hu Jintao era (2003) and capture 4 years of the Xi Jinping era to provide a basis for comparison. Another reason for the start date is some key sources, such as *China Vitae,* do not cover activities before 2003.

[2] The Chinese version of *Jiefangjun Bao* (JFJB) or *Liberation Army Daily* (LAD) can be found at <www.chinamil.com.cn/>, and the English version at <english.chinamil.com.cn/>.

[3] *China Armed Forces* has been published since January 2009 by Xinhua News Agency's military department. It was published quarterly from 2009 to 2011 and has been produced bimonthly since then.

[4] The People's Liberation Army (PLA) is not consistent in how it translates *guofang bu* (国防部). Although it normally uses "Ministry of National Defense," it also uses "Defense Ministry" and "Ministry of Defense." It also uses the initialisms MND and MOD.

[5] Information Office of the State Council, "The Diversified Employment of China's Armed Forces," April 2013, People's Republic of China Ministry of Defense, available in English at <http://eng.mod.gov.cn/TopNews/2013-04/16/content_4442750.htm>. The Chinese version is available at <www.mod.gov.cn/affair/2013-04/16/content_4442839.htm>.

[6] Andrew S. Erickson and Austin M. Strange, *No Substitute for Experience: Chinese Antipiracy Operations in the Gulf of Aden* (Newport, RI: U.S. Naval War College, 2013).

[7] Although the former name was the General Logistics Department, the new name uses Logistic instead of Logistics. See Zhang Tao, "China Establishes Joint Logistic Support Force," *China Military Online*, September 13, 2016, available at <http://eng.chinamil.com.cn/view/2016-09/13/content_7256651.htm>.

[8] For an analysis and details on the reorganization, see Joel Wuthnow and Phillip C. Saunders, *Chinese Military Reform in the Age of Xi Jinping*, China Strategic Perspective 10 (Washington, DC: NDU Press, 2017), available at <http://ndupress.ndu.edu/Portals/68/Documents/stratperspective/china/ChinaPerspectives-10.pdf?ver=2017-03-21-152018-430>.

[9] The authors thank Joel Wuthnow for pointing this out.

[10] Gu Dexin, ed., *International Military Relations*, vol. 1[国际军事关系 (学科分册I)] (Beijing: Encyclopedia of China Publishing House, 2007), 1.

[11] All-Military Military Affairs Management Committee [全军军事管理委员会], ed., *PLA Military Terminology* [中华人民解放军军语] (Beijing: Academy of Military Sciences Press, 2011), 1063.

[12] Ibid., 7–10; Zhou Congbao and Zhong Hai, eds., *On Strategy for Military Diplomacy* [军事外交战略学] (Beijing: National Defense University Press [NDU], 2015), 7.

[13] Gu, Dexin, 1.

[14] Chu Yongzheng, ed., *Military Diplomacy* [军事外交学] (Beijing: NDU Press, 2015), 117–125.

[15] Ibid., 125–131.

[16] Ibid., 133, 137–141.

[17] Yang Lina and Chang Xuemei, eds., "Xi Jinping: Start a New Phase of Military Diplomacy [习近平：进一步开创军事外交新局面]," Xinhua, January 29, 2015, available at <http://cpc.people.com.cn/n/2015/0129/c64094-26474947.html>.

[18] Jin Canrong and Wang Bo, "On Theory of Military Diplomacy with Chinese Characteristics [有关中国特色军事外交的理论思考]," *Pacific Studies Report* [太平洋学报] no. 5 (2015), 22, available at <www.cssn.cn/jsx/201601/P020160104312124234558.pdf>; Wan Fayang, *Chinese Military Diplomacy—Theory and Practice* [中国军事外交理论与实践] (Beijing: Current Affairs Press, 2015), 294–309; Chen Zhiyong, "Retrospect and Thinking of the 60 Years of Military Diplomacy in New China [新中国60年军事外交回顾与思考]," *China Military Science* [中国军事科学] 5 (2009), 35–36; "Chinese Military Diplomacy and Military Messaging to the Outside [中国军事外交中的军事对外传播]," *PLA Daily*, January 2, 2014, available at <www.81.cn/jkhc/2014-01/02/content_5716684.htm>.

[19] Wan Fayang, 294–309.

[20] For an overview of the geographical distribution of Chinese foreign policy interests, see Phillip C. Saunders, *China's Global Activism: Strategy, Drivers, and Tools* (Washington, DC: NDU Press, 2006).

[21] China's Asia-Pacific white paper provides numerous examples of the role of military diplomacy in advancing China's regional policy and relations with the United States and Russia. See State Council Information Office, "China's Policies on Asia-Pacific Security Cooperation," January 11, 2017.

[22] Peter Cai, *Understanding China's Belt and Road Initiative* (Sydney: Lowy Institute, 2017), available at <www.lowyinstitute.org/publications/understanding-belt-and-road-initiative>.

[23] Ibid., 181.

[24] Li Lu and Li Jing, "'Peace Mission' Is Deeply and Broadly Meaningful [和平使命 军演意义深远]," *PLA Daily*, September 5, 2014, available at <www.81.cn/jwgd/2014-09/05/content_6125535.htm>.

[25] Information Office of the State Council, "China's Military Strategy," May 2015, People's Republic of China Ministry of Defense, available at <http://eng.mod.gov.cn/Database/WhitePapers/2015-05/26/content_4586715.htm>.

[26] Wan Fayang, 312, 348; Huang Zijuan and Yan Jiaqi, "Expert: PLA Navy Ships Exercise in the South China Sea to Display the Achievements of PLA Military Construction [海军三大舰队南海演习，专家：展示中国军队建设成就]," *People's Daily*, July 11, 2016, available at <http://military.people.com.cn/n1/2016/0711/c1011-28543175.html>.

[27] Wan Fayang, 315.

[28] "China's Military Strategy"; Information Office of the State Council, "The Diversified Employment of China's Armed Forces."

[29] "'Aviadarts 2014' International Pilot Competition Ends," *China Military Online*, July 29, 2014, available at http://eng.mod.gov.cn/Photos/2014-07/29/content_4525343.htm.; Yao Jianing, "Ma Xiaotian Meets with Portuguese Air Force Chief of Staff," *China Military Online*, December 9, 2014, available at <http://english.chinamil.com.cn/news-channels/china-military-news/2014-12/09/content_6261756.htm>.

[30] China does not have *allies* in the Western sense of the term.

[31] Wan Fayang, 326.

[32] Zhang Tao, "China, Pakistan Launch Joint Air Drill," *China Military Online*, September 6, 2015, available at <http://english.chinamil.com.cn/news-channels/china-military-news/2015-09/06/content_6667497.htm>; Ayaz Gul, "China Delivers First Batch of Military Aid to Afghanistan," Voice of America, July 3, 2016, available at <www.voanews.com/content/china-military-aid-afghanistan/3402178.html>.

[33] Wan Fayang, 312.

[34] This position, currently held by Admiral Sun Jianguo, was the Deputy Chief of General Staff with the intelligence and foreign affairs portfolio prior to the PLA reforms announced in January 2016.

[35] "China's Military Strategy."

[36] Ministry of Foreign Affairs of the People's Republic of China, "The Third Round of China-Germany Foreign Ministers' Strategic Dialogue to Be Held Soon," October 9, 2012, available at <www.fmprc.gov.cn/mfa_eng/wjdt_665385/wsrc_665395/t978502.shtml>.

[37] The Xiangshan Forum is co-sponsored by the China Institute for International Studies (a Foreign Ministry think tank) and the China Association for Military Science (a nominally independent association headed by the president of the PLA's Academy of Military Sciences).

[38] Zhang Tao, "Defense Ministry's Regular Press Conference on Dec. 25, 2014," Ministry of National Defense, December 25, 2014, available at <http://english.chinamil.com.cn/news-channels/2014-12/25/content_6284814.htm>.

[39] Information Office of the State Council, "The Diversified Employment of China's Armed Forces"; Zhang Tao, "Aviadarts 2014 International Pilot Competition Ends," *China Military Online*, July 29, 2014, available at <http://eng.mod.gov.cn/Photos/2014-07/29/content_4525343.htm>.

[40] Wan Fayang, 313.

[41] Erickson and Strange.

[42] Whereas Western English-language articles use *escort task force*, China's English-language articles from sources such as Xinhua, *China Armed Forces*, and *China Military Online* use *escort taskforce*. An official brochure published by the People's Republic of China's (PRC's) International Communication Bureau of the Ministry of National Defense (国防部国际传播局) titled *Escort Operations of the Chinese PLA Navy* use *convoy task force* and the acronym *CTF*. For purposes of this paper, escort task force (ETF) is used.

[43] Fang Lihua and Ju Zhenhua, "Spreading Friendship and Compassion to 16 Nations and Tempering Capabilities While Journeying Across the Worlds' Oceans—Peace Ark: The Impressive Calling Card for a Responsible Nation [倾情播撒友谊爱播十六国眠断能力航迹遍及工三洋—和平方舟：负责任大国形象的亮丽名片]," *Renmin Haijun*, November 1, 2013; Shihar Aneez and Ranga Sirilal, "Chinese Submarine Docks in Sri Lanka Despite Indian concerns," Reuters, November 2, 2014, available at <www.reuters.com/article/us-sri-lanka-china-submarine-idUSKBN0IM0LY20141102>.

[44] Wan Fayang, 314–319.

[45] Yao Jianing, "Ma Xiaotian Meets with Portuguese Air Force Chief of Staff"; John S. Van Oudenaren and Benjamin E. Fisher, "Foreign Military Education as PLA Soft Power," *Parameters* 46, no. 4 (Winter 2016–2017), 105–118.

[46] "China's Military Strategy"; see also Du Nongyi and Wang Tao, "Peacekeeping Diplomacy: Main Theme of Military Diplomacy in the New Phase of the New Century [维和外交：新世纪新阶段军事外交的主旋律]," *China Military Science* [中国军事科学] 4 (2007), 109–111.

[47] Zhang Tao, "China Sends First Infantry Battalion for UN Peacekeeping," Xinhua, December 22, 2014, available at <http://english.chinamil.com.cn/news-channels/2014-12/22/content_6280182.htm>; Erickson and Strange; Qiang Lijing, "Timeline: China's Military in the Search for MH370," *China Armed Forces* 2, no. 26 (2014), 12–17; Meng Jinyu, "Aerial Search for MH370 [空中搜寻MH370]," *China Air Force*, April 2014, 36–38.

[48] The PLA's participation in strategic dialogues is grouped with senior-level meetings and visits, as information on the meetings held by senior PLA leaders often did not confirm whether the meeting was held as part of a dialogue.

[49] Although China's official media uses *Minister of National Defense* and *Defense Minister* for its leader (国防部部长), this paper uses *Defense Minister*. See Yao Jianing, "Four Meetings Between Chinese and U.S. Naval Chiefs in One Year," *China Military Online*, September 18, 2014, available at <http://eng.chinamil.com.cn/news-channels/china-military-news/2014-09/18/content_6144343.htm>; Yao Jianing, "Wu Shengli Flies to U.S. for International Seapower Symposium," *China Military Online*, September 16, 2014, available at <http://eng.chinamil.com.cn/news-channels/china-military-news/2014-09/16/content_6140003.htm>.

[50] Other PLA leaders also sometimes interact with foreigners, but on a much less regular basis.

[51] One of these areas is national defense mobilization. The Defense Minister serves as a vice chairman of the National Defense Mobilization Committee (国家国防动员委员会), established in 1994 under the dual control of the CMC and State Council. The other notable military representative on this committee is DCOGS Admiral Sun Jianguo, whose portfolio includes defense mobilization. The Defense Minister's position as a State Councilor provides him with the appropriate status in the state system to participate in cabinet executive meetings, though his status is probably informally greater than other State Councilors because he represents the CMC, which is an organization of the same weight as the State Council. For more, see Kenneth W. Allen et al., "China's Defense Minister and Ministry of National Defense," in *The PLA as Organization v2.0*, ed. Kevin Pollpeter and Kenneth Allen, (Vienna, VA: Defense Group, Inc., 2015).

[52] PLA Air Force Commander General Ma Xiaotian traveled extensively while serving as the DCOGS in charge of foreign affairs and intelligence and did not want to travel abroad, according to information from various interviews conducted by the author.

[53] For instance, Beijing Military Region commander Zhang Shibo (张仕波) led a delegation to the United States in November 2013, and Chengdu MR PC Zhu Fuxi hosted Thailand's acting Vice Minister of Defense, who was en route to attend the 10th China-Thailand Defense and Security Consultations in Beijing in June 2014. See Xu Hongcai, "Zhu Fuxi Meets Thailand's Acting Vice Defense Ministry [朱福熙会见泰国国防部代理次长]," *Zhanqi Bao*, June 16, 2014, 1.

[54] United States Air Force, "Nanjing Regional Air Force Command Visits Pacific Air Forces," September 25, 2014, available at <http://www.pacaf.af.mil/News/ArticleDisplay/tabid/377/Article/591140/nanjing-regional-air-force-command-visits-pacific-air-forces.aspx>.

[55] Senior PLA leadership included CMC members, designated deputy General Department leaders, National Defense University (NDU) and Academy of Military Science leaders as well as political commissars, military region commanders and political commissars, and designated assistants to General Department leaders for which media reporting was available.

[56] On occasion, when foreign military leaders meet with their PLA counterparts, they also meet separately with other senior PLA officers. These separate meetings are included in this dataset. PLA leaders who accompany senior civilian leaders to foreign countries are not counted as separate visits because these personnel are not heads of delegation.

[57] The year 2007 is a slight anomaly, probably because the CCP General Secretary (Hu Jintao)

and the two CMC Vice Chairs (Xu Caihou and Guo Boxiong) all stayed on for a second term. This reduced the need for senior PLA officers to stay at home to lobby for promotions.

[58] Authors' interactions with PLA delegations.

[59] The term *joint* is a term used in PRC English-language media. Chinese media use 联合, which can mean *combined*, *combined arms*, and *joint* in U.S. military parlance.

[60] Information Office of the State Council, "The Diversified Employment of China's Armed Forces." See also Zhang Tao, "Chinese and Indonesian Special Operation Forces Hold Joint Training," *China Military Online*, July 2, 2012, available at <http://eng.chinamil.com.cn/news-channels/china-military-news/2012-07/02/content_4920071.htm>; and Chen Jie, "China, Thailand Hold Anti-Terrorism Training," Xinhua, December 9, 2013, available at <http://eng.chinamil.com.cn/news-channels/china-military-news/2013-12/09/content_5683020.htm>.

[61] See Guo Renjie, "PLA to Debut in U.S.-Thailand Military Exercise," Xinhua, February 11, 2014, available at <http://eng.chinamil.com.cn/news-channels/china-military-news/2014-02/11/content_5764942.htm>; and Li Xiaokun and Mo Jingxi, "China Joins U.S.-Thailand Drill," *China Daily*, February 12, 2014, available at <http://usa.chinadaily.com.cn/world/2014-02/12/content_17277823.htm>.

[62] "Chinese Troop Joins ASEAN Humanitarian Assistance, Disaster-Relief Exercise," Xinhua, April 29, 2014, available at <http://news.xinhuanet.com/english/china/2014-04/29/c_133296424.htm>.

[63] Yao Jianing, "Chinese Soldiers Join Australian, U.S. Troops in Joint Exercises in Australia," Xinhua, October 8, 2014, available at <http://eng.mod.gov.cn/DefenseNews/2014-10/08/content_4541775.htm>.

[64] Zhang Tao, "China-Mongolia Joint Military Training for Disaster Relief Ends," *China Military Online*, September 24, 2013, available at <http://eng.chinamil.com.cn/news-channels/photo-reports/2013-09/24/content_5533347.htm>.

[65] Li Fenfen, "Pakistan Hosts 'Peace Angel-2014' Combined Humanitarian Assistance and Disaster Relief Exercise [中巴举行和平天使-2014联合卫勤演练]," Xinhua, April 19, 2014, available at <http://news.mod.gov.cn/headlines/2014-04/19/content_4504223.htm>. See also Guo Renjie, "'Peace Angel 2014' China-Pakistan Joint Medical Exercise Concludes," *China Military Online*, April 28, 2014, available at <http://eng.chinamil.com.cn/news-channels/china-military-news/2014-04/28/content_5883969.htm>.

[66] See Guo Renjie, "Chinese Military Exercises Create Records in 2014," *China Military Online*, December 17, 2014, available at <http://english.chinamil.com.cn/news-channels/china-military-news/2014-12/17/content_6273930.htm>; Zhang Tao, "Chinese Tanks Appear in International Tank Competition," *China Military Online*, August 5, 2014, available at <http://english.chinamil.com.cn/news-channels/photo-reports/2014-08/05/content_6080294.htm>; "Russia Wins World Championship Tank Biathlon 2014," *Russia Today*, August 16, 2014, available at <http://rt.com/in-motion/180820-final-russia-tank-biathlon/>; Guo Renjie, "Made-in-China Armored Equipment Debuts in Tank Biathlon-2014," *China Military Online*, October 23, 2014, available at <http://eng.chinamil.com.cn/news-channels/photo-reports/2014-10/23/content_6192140.htm>; Miles Yu, "Tanked in Russia," *Washington Times*, August 21, 2014, available at <www.washingtontimes.com/news/2014/aug/21/inside-china-tanked-in-russia/?page=all>.

[67] Information Office of the State Council, "The Diversified Employment of China's Armed

Forces"; Fang Yang, "Marine Forces of China, Thailand to Hold Joint Training," *Xinhua*, May 8, 2012, available at <http://news.xinhuanet.com/english/china/2012-05/08/c_131575846.htm>.

[68] "China, U.S. Successfully Stage Joint Maritime SAREX," *Crienglish.com*, November 12, 2013, available at <http://english.cri.cn/11354/2013/11/12/3481s797984.htm>.

[69] Ibid.

[70] Zhang Tao, "Chinese Fleet Joins Others for RIMPAC Exercise," *Xinhua*, June 14, 2014, available at <http://eng.chinamil.com.cn/news-channels/china-military-news/2014-06/14/content_5960521.htm>.

[71] Zachary Keck, "U.S. Welcomes China's RIMPAC Spying," *The Diplomat*, July 30, 2014, available at <http://thediplomat.com/2014/07/us-welcomes-chinas-rimpac-spying/>.

[72] Jane Perlez, "U.S. Naval Ties with China Advance, Symbolically," *New York Times*, July 20, 2014, available at <http://sinosphere.blogs.nytimes.com/2014/07/20/u-s-naval-ties-with-china-advance-symbolically/?_r=0>.

[73] Rear Admiral Frederick J. Roegge, "RIMPAC 2016: An Exercise in Response and Interoperability," *Navy Live Blog*, July 29, 2016, available at <http://navylive.dodlive.mil/2016/07/29/rimpac-2016-an-exercise-in-response-and-interoperability/>.

[74] Guo Renjie, "'Komodo' Multilateral Humanitarian Rescue Maritime Actual-Troop Drill Concluded," *China Military Online*, April 2, 2014, available at <http://eng.chinamil.com.cn/news-channels/photo-reports/2014-04/02/content_5837820.htm>.

[75] Note that the exercises have also been identified as joint sea exercises. *China Armed Forces* has an article that identifies the exercise as Joint-Sea 2014. See Cao Kai, "A Record of 'Joint-Sea 2014' [海上联合-2014演习全记录]," *China Armed Forces* 3, no. 27 (2014), 14–23. To further confuse the situation, the PLA Navy (PLAN) held a combined exercise on April 23, 2014, near Qingdao in conjunction with its 65th anniversary and Western Pacific Naval Symposium–2014 that was also identified in English as Maritime Cooperation–2014; however, the Chinese characters are different (海上合作). See Wang Jingguo, "Maritime Cooperation 2014 [海上合作-2014]," *China Armed Forces* 3, no. 27 (2014), 60–65.

[76] The use of sensors and communications devices in an exercise allows the foreign partner to collect information on the ranges and frequencies of such systems, which is valuable technical intelligence. See "Chinese Military Exercises Create Records in 2014," *China Military Online*, December 17, 2014, available at <http://english.chinamil.com.con/news-channels/china-militay-news/2014-12/17/content_6273930.htm>.

[77] For an assessment of these exercises and of Sino-Russia military cooperation more generally, see Richard Weitz, *Parsing Chinese-Russian Military Exercises* (Carlisle, PA: Strategic Studies Institute, 2015).

[78] Ben Blanchard, "China, Russia to Hold First Joint Mediterranean Naval Drills in May," Reuters, April 30, 2015, available at <www.reuters.com/article/us-china-russia-military-idUSKBN0NL16F20150430>.

[79] Jeffrey Lin and P.W. Singer, "The Chinese-Russian South China Sea Naval Exercises: What Happened and Why Did It Matter?" *Eastern Arsenal Blog*, September 21, 2016, available at <www.popsci.com/chinese-russian-south-china-sea-naval-exercises-what-happened-and-why-did-it-matter>.

[80] Zhang Qiliang, *Naval Diplomacy Theory* [海军外交论] (Beijing: Academy of Military Science Press, 2011), 243.

[81] Kenneth Allen, "China's Air Force Foreign Relations Program and Implications for Interaction with the U.S. Air Force," *Foreign Area Office Association Journal of International Affairs*, March 3, 2015.

[82] Zhao Lei, "PLA Air Force Seeks Collaboration," *China Daily*, September 24, 2014, available at <www.chinadaily.com.cn/china/2014-09/24/content_18649783.htm>.

[83] Ouyang Dongmei, "Chinese and Pakistani Air Forces Hold Joint Training," *China Military Online*, September 23, 2013, available at <http://eng.chinamil.com.cn/news-channels/photo-reports/2013-09/23/content_5527605.htm>.

[84] Ibid.

[85] Yao Jianing, "Ma Xiaotian Meets with Portuguese Air Force Chief of Staff."

[86] "Chinese, Belarusian Airborne Troops Hold Joint Exercise in China," Xinhua, November 27, 2012, available at <http://english.peopledaily.com.cn/90786/8035739.html>. See also "China-Belarus 'Condor 2012' Joint Anti-Terrorism Training Wrapped Up," *China Military Online*, December 6, 2012, available at <http://eng.chinamil.com.cn/special-reports/2007zgjdgjtm/2012-12/06/content_5140507.htm>; Zhang Xuefeng, "The Thunderers [雷神突击队]," *China Armed Forces* 3, no. 15 (2012), 42–47.

[87] "China, Indonesia Airborne Troops Complete Anti-Terrorism Exercise," Xinhua, November 11, 2013, available at <www.globaltimes.cn/content/824095.shtml#.UvPw2P0ZIYV>. This was a follow-up to Sharp Knife 2011 in Bandong, Indonesia, and Sharp Knife 2012 in Jinan, China. See Jiang Fan, "China-Indonesia Joint Training for Special Forces Ends in Bandung," *People's Daily*, June 18, 2011, available at <http://english.peopledaily.com.cn/90001/90776/90883/7413666.html>. Each of these involved special forces. Guo Renjie, "Chinese, Indonesian Airborne Forces Hold Joint Anti-Terror Drill," *China Military Online*, October 27, 2014, available at <http://eng.mod.gov.cn/DefenseNews/2014-10/27/content_4547351.htm>.

[88] "Russian Airborne Troops to Visit China for Skills Exchange," Xinhua, May 27, 2014, available at <www.chinadaily.com.cn/china/2014-05/27/content_17545229.htm>.

[89] Zhang Tao, "Aviadarts 2014 International Pilot Competition Ends," *China Military Online*, July 29, 2014, available at <http://eng.mod.gov.cn/Photos/2014-07/29/content_4525343.htm>.

[90] While three Su-30s and six pilots deployed to Russia, it appears that only two aircraft and four pilots participated.

[91] Fang Yang, "'Peace Mission–2009' Improves Anti-Terror Response: Chinese Military Officer," Xinhua, July 24, 2009, available at <http://news.Xinhuanet.com/english/2009-07/24/content_11765127.htm>; Du Mingming and Zhang Qian, "Backgrounder: China-Russia Joint Military Exercises Since 2003," Xinhua, July 6, 2013, available at <http://english.peopledaily.com.cn/90786/8313722.html>.

[92] Lian Junyi et al., eds., "Agenda," in *Peace Mission-2010*, *China Military Online*, available at <http://eng.mod.gov.cn/SpecialReports/SCO%20Joint%20Military%20Exercises.htm>; Yang Lina, "Peace Mission 2010 Concludes, Opens New Page for SCO Cooperation," Xinhua, September 25, 2010, available at <http://news.Xinhuanet.com/english2010/world/2010-09/25/c_13529321.htm>; Roger McDermott, "PLA Displays Network-Centric Capabilities in Peace Mission 2010," *Eurasia Daily Monitor* 7, no. 180 (October 6, 2010), available at available at <www.jamestown.org/programs/edm/single/?tx_ttnews%5Btt_news%5D=37001&cHash=ff5fd5240d#.U_oxmbl0y9I>.

[93] *China Military Online* hosted an official English-language Web site (http://eng.chinamil.com.cn/special-reports/node_60757.htm) devoted solely to Peace Mission–2013, which also had links to the

previous exercises. Several other Chinese and Russian English-language articles provided information about the exercise. See also Pavel Lisicin, "Peace Mission 2013 Russian-Chinese Anti-Terror Exercise," *RIA Novosti*, August 14, 2013, available at <http://en.ria.ru/photolents/20130814/182739162/Peace-Mission-2013-Russian-Chinese-Anti-Terror-Exercise.html>; Liu Dan, "Peace Mission–2013 China-Russia Joint Drill Ends," Xinhua, August 16, 2013, available at <http://news.Xinhuanet.com/english/video/2013-08/16/c_132635278.htm>; "'Peace Mission-2013': China-Russia Relations in New Context," ITAR-TASS News Service, August 20, 2013, available at <http://rbth.asia/world/2013/08/20/peace_mission-2013_china-russia_relations_in_new_context_48549.html>; Tan Changjun, "China Carries Out 1st Reconnaissance Mission in Joint Military Drills," *Global Times*, August 7, 2013, available at <www.globaltimes.cn/content/802152.shtml>.

[94] See Guo Renjie, "Joint Tactical Coordination Conducted in Peace Mission–2014 Exercise," *China Military Online*, August 22, 2014, available at <http://eng.chinamil.com.cn/news-channels/china-military-news/2014-08/22/content_6107131.htm>; Yao Jianing, "PLA Air Force Troops in 'Peace Mission–2014' Show Four Main Features," *China Military Online*, August 21, 2014, available at <http://eng.chinamil.com.cn/news-channels/china-military-news/2014-08/21/content_6105578.htm>; Zhang Tao, "Chinese Troops Participating in 'Peace Mission–2014' Take Mass Pledge in Zhurihe," *China Military Online*, August 7, 2014, available at <http://eng.chinamil.com.cn/news-channels/china-military-news/2014-08/07/content_6084068.htm>; "SCO Exercise Peace Mission 2014 to Involve 7,000 Troops," ITAR-TASS News Agency, August 19, 2014, available at <http://en.ITAR-TASS.com/world/745617>; Wang Xu, "Joint Military Drill to Hone Anti-Terror Capacity," *China Daily*, August 19, 2014, available at <http://usa.chinadaily.com.cn/china/2014-08/19/content_18444004.htm>; Yao Jianing, "Ten Breakthroughs of China's Military Diplomacy in 2014 (1)," *China Military Online*, December 26, 2014, available at <http://english.chinamil.com.cn/news-channels/2014-12/26/content_6286046.htm>.

[95] Paul Goble, "Military Suffering Casualties in War Games," *Moscow Times*, August 12, 2009, available at <www.militaryphotos.net/forums/showthread.php?163042-Bad-maps-kill-60-Chinese-15-Russian-soldiers-during-Peace-Mission-2009>.

[96] Zhu Yingqiu et al., eds., "About Peace Mission 2012," *China Military Online*, June 8, 2014, available at <http://eng.chinamil.com.cn/special-reports/node_54180.htm>; Roger N. McDermott, "SCO 'Peace Mission' 2012 Promotes Security Myths," FOI Memo 4040, July 2012, available at <www.foi.se/Global/V%C3%A5r%20kunskap/S%C3%A4kerhetspolitiska%20studier/Ryssland/Briefings/RUFS%20Briefing%20No.%2014%20-%2012070>; Martin Andrew, "Power Politics: China, Russia, and Peace Mission 2005," *China Brief* 5, no. 20 (September 2005).

[97] This paper defines *exercises* as maneuvers that the PLA had a hand in planning, and *exercise interactions* as the number of times the PLA interacted with a foreign country in the context of military exercises, including those that the Chinese had no role in planning.

[98] Authors' interview with a PLA flag officer, 2014.

[99] "Chinese Military Exercises Create Records in 2014," *China Military Online*, December 17, 2014, available at <http://english.chinamil.com.con/news-channels/china-militay-news/2014-12/17/content_6273930.htm>. See the PLA Army's performance at the Tank Biathlon 2014 competition.

[100] Zhang Tao, "Defense Ministry's Regular Press Conference on Dec. 25, 2014."

101 Lin and Singer.

102 Zhang Tao, "Defense Ministry's Regular Press Conference on Dec. 25, 2014."

103 Good examples of a replenishment visit include Wu Di, "Chinese Naval Ship Berths in Salalah Port for Replenishment," *China Military Online*, October 8, 2014, available at <http://eng.mod.gov.cn/HomePicture/2014-10/08/content_4542110.htm>; and Yao Jianing, "Chinese Naval Escort Taskforce Stops at Djibouti Port for Replenishment and Rest," *China Military Online*, September 9, 2014, available at <http://eng.chinamil.com.cn/news-channels/china-military-news/2014-09/09/content_6129544.htm>.

104 Good examples of a friendly visit include Zhang Tao, "Chinese Naval Escort Taskforce Docks in Singapore," *China Military Online*, October 13, 2014, available at <http://eng.mod.gov.cn/DefenseNews/2014-10/13/content_4543084.htm>.

105 Yan Meng and Yao Chun, "CTF 151 Commander Visits 14th Chinese Naval Escort Task-force," *People's Daily*, May 8, 2013, available at <http://en.people.cn/90786/8235569.html>.

106 Guo Renjie, "Chinese Escort Taskforce Commanding Officer Meets with Singaporean Counterpart," *China Military Online*, June 11, 2014, available at <http://eng.chinamil.com.cn/news-channels/china-military-news/2014-06/11/content_5953400.htm>.

107 Li Youping, "European Union Navy 46th Task Force Command Officers Visits the Changchun Vessel [欧盟海军465编队指挥官访问长春舰]," *Renmin Haijun*, July 4, 2014.

108 Lu Yu, "Commentary: Closer Military Cooperation Conducive to Improving China-U.S. Mutual Trust," Xinhua, August 24, 2013, available at <http://news.xinhuanet.com/english/indepth/2013-08/24/c_132659450.htm>; Chen Lin, "Joint Sea Drill Shows Improved Relations," *China Daily*, August 26, 2013, available at <http://usa.chinadaily.com.cn/china/2013-08/26/content_16919254.htm>; Deng Xiguang, Wang Changsong, and Cai Zengbing, "A Sino-U.S. Joint Anti-Piracy Drill," *China Armed Forces* 5, no. 23 (2013), 23–25.

109 Wang Changsong, Qin Chuan, and Li Ding, "'Peace-13' Joint Maritime Drill [和平-13 多国海上联合演习]," *China Armed Forces* 2, no. 20 (2013), 42–47.

110 Guo Renjie, "Chinese and Nigerian Navies Conduct First Anti-Piracy Joint Drill," *China Military Online*, May 29, 2014, available at <http://eng.chinamil.com.cn/news-channels/china-military-news/2014-05/29/content_5923490.htm>; Guo Renjie, "Chinese Naval Fleet Pays First Visit to Cameroon," *China Military Online*, June 3, 2014, available at <http://eng.chinamil.com.cn/news-channels/china-military-news/2014-06/03/content_5932926.htm>.

111 Rong Junjie, Li Xiao, and Hu Quanfu, "First Sino-European Anti-Piracy Drill," *China Armed Forces* 2, no. 26 (2014), 8, 83–85.

112 Zhang Tao, "China, Iran to Stage Joint Navy Drills in Persian Gulf," *Global Times*, September 23, 2014, available at <http://eng.chinamil.com.cn/news-channels/china-military-news/2014-09/23/content_6150650.htm>.

113 Zeng Xingjian and Hong Yihu, "Passing the Strait of Magellan," *China Armed Forces* 6, no. 24 (2013), 80–83.

114 Dong Zhaohui, "Chinese 'Changxing Island' Submarine Support Ship in Colombo Port of Sri Lanka," *China Military Online*, September 24, 2014, available at <http://eng.chinamil.com.cn/news-channels/china-military-news/2014-09/24/content_6152669.htm>.

115 Dong Zhaohui, "Dutch Expert: Sending Submarine by China for Escort Beyond Reproach,"

China Military Online, September 29, 2014, available at <http://eng.chinamil.com.cn/news-channels/china-military-news/2014-09/29/content_6160307.htm>.

[116] The PLAN also has another training ship, the Type 0891A *Shichang* (82), which was commissioned in January 1997. The *Shichang* is primarily used for surface navigation and helicopter training. It has also participated in task force visits to various countries, including Australia in 1998, and naval exercises. See Bernard D. Cole, *The Great Wall at Sea: China's Navy in the Twenty-first Century* (Annapolis, MD: Naval Institute Press, 2010), 132.

[117] Zhang Xiaomin, "Naval Training Ship Going Round the Globe," *China Daily*, April 17, 2012, available at <www.china.org.cn/china/2012-04/17/content_25160837.htm>.

[118] Dong Zhaohui, "Naval Training Taskforce Commander: 'High-sea Training Voyage Reaps a Lot,'" *China Military Online*, June 25, 2014, available at <http://eng.chinamil.com.cn/news-channels/china-military-news/2014-06/25/content_6010970.htm>; Yao Jianing, "Chinese Training Ship Taskforce Wraps Up Visit to Indonesia," Ministry of Defense, June 9, 2014, available at <http://eng.mod.gov.cn/DefenseNews/2014-06/09/content_4514963.htm>. The vessels were originally scheduled to visit Vietnam but apparently switched to Singapore while at sea.

[119] Some PLAN ships conducted port calls during military exercises with other countries, as one ship did during a 2012 exercise with Russia. The reporting on these port calls did not always specify if a port call occurred as a part of a military exercise.

[120] The PLA does not have a term that translates directly as professional military education. The closest term is *peixun* (培训), which is a combination of *peiyang* (培养) and *xunlian* (训练). PLA dictionaries translate *peiyang* as development and training, training, or cultivation and training. See Dong Huiyu and Mou Xianming, eds., *Dictionary of Modern Military Education*, 2nd ed. [现代军校教育辞典] (Beijing: National Defense University Press, August 2011), 223; *China's PLA Military Terminology* (中国人民解放军军语) (Beijing: Academy of Military Science Press, December 2011), 323.

[121] See Eric Hagt, "The Rise of PLA Diplomacy," in *PLA Influence on China's National Security Policymaking*, ed. Phillip C. Saunders and Andrew Scobell (Stanford: Stanford University Press, 2015), 218–248.

[122] Van Oudenaren and Fisher, 105–118.

[123] Chu Zhenjiang and Luo Jinmu, "National Defense University Strengthens Strategic Cooperation with Several Countries' Well-Known Academic Institutions [国防大学与多国名校加强战略合作]," *PLA Daily*, May 12, 2014.

[124] "Courses," College of Defence Studies Web site, available at <www.cdsndu.org/html_en/to_columnContent_orderNo=2402&superOrderNo=2400.html>.

[125] Guo Renjie, "National Defense University of PLA Awards Master Degree to Foreign Senior Officers," *China Military Online*, September 9, 2014, available at <http://eng.chinamil.com.cn/news-channels/china-military-news/2014-09/09/content_6129447.htm>.

[126] Lin Peixiong, Liu Demao, and Tao Shelan, "College of Defense Studies' Top Secret: 4,000 Foreign Military Officers Trained Already [国防大学防务学院首次揭秘：已培训4千多名外国军官]," Xinhua, September 5, 2010, available at <http://news.xinhuanet.com/school/2010-09/05/c_12519388.htm>.

[127] Yan Meng and Yao Chun, "5th International Cadets Week Unveiled at PLA University of

Science and Technology," *China Military Online*, November 4, 2013, available at <http://english.people.com.cn/90786/8445306.html>.

[128] Yu Hongchun, "Opening: Flying High and Far in Confidence [开放：在自信中高飞远航]," *China Air Force*, November 2014, 28–29.

[129] Yao Jianing, "Ma Xiaotian Meets with Portuguese Air Force Chief of Staff."

[130] Guo Kai and Wang Caishan, "Air Force Command College Grants 20 Foreign Students Master's Degree [空军指挥学院授予20名外军留学生硕士学位]," *Air Force News*, July 17, 2014, 1.

[131][130] Feng Guoxiong, "China and Foreign Army Academic Institution Presidents Hold Discussions and Exchanges [中外陆军院校长研讨交流活动举行]," *PLA Daily*, November 7, 2013.

[132] David Shambaugh, *China Goes Global: The Partial Power* (New York: Oxford University Press, 2013), 301.

[133] Information Office of the State Council, "The Diversified Employment of China's Armed Forces."

[134] Zhang Tao, "China Sends First Infantry Battalion for UN Peacekeeping," Xinhua, December 22, 2014, available at <http://english.chinamil.com.cn/news-channels/2014-12/22/content_6280182.htm>.

[135] "China to Replace Japan as Second-Largest Funder of U.N. Peacekeeping," *Japan Times*, December 22, 2015, available at <www.japantimes.co.jp/news/2015/12/22/national/politics-diplomacy/china-replace-japan-second-largest-funder-u-n-peacekeeping/#.WMm64fIsDZv>.

[136] See United Nations (UN), "UN Mission's Summary Detailed by Country: Month of Report: 31-Jan-17," January 31, 2017, available at <www.un.org/en/peacekeeping/contributors/2017/jan17_3.pdf>.

[137] "News," *China Armed Forces* 4, no. 22 (2013), 6.

[138] Zhang Tao, "China Sends First Infantry Battalion for UN Peacekeeping"; Yao Jianing, "China to Send First Infantry Battalion for UN Peacekeeping," *China Daily*, December 23, 2014, available at <http://english.chinamil.com.cn/news-channels/2014-12/23/content_6281041.htm>.

[139] Yang Lina, "Multinational Peacekeeping Exercise Begins in Mongolia," Xinhua, August 12, 2012, available at <http://news.Xinhuanet.com/english/world/2012-08/12/c_131779809.htm>.

[140] Zhang Tao, "China Trains Foreign Peacekeepers," Xinhua, June 16, 2014, available at <http://eng.chinamil.com.cn/news-channels/china-military-news/2014-06/16/content_5966206.htm>.

[141] International Crisis Group, *China's Growing Role in UN Peacekeeping*, Asia Report No. 166, International Crisis Group, April 17, 2009, 1, available at <www.voltairenet.org/IMG/pdf/China_and_UN_Peacekeeping.pdf>.

[142] Yao Jianing, "UN Military Observers Course Begins in Beijing," *China Military Online*, September 2, 2014, available at <http://eng.chinamil.com.cn/news-channels/china-military-news/2014-09/02/content_6121898.htm>.

[143] "News," *China Armed Forces* 5, no. 23 (2013), 6.

[144] See Courtney J. Fung, *China's Troop Contributions to U.N. Peacekeeping*, Peacebrief 212, July 26, 2016, available at <www.usip.org/publications/2016/07/chinas-troop-contributions-un-peacekeeping>.

[145] Authors' interview with UN peacekeeping official, October 2016.

146 Colum Lynch, "China Eyes Ending Western Grip on Top U.N. Jobs with Greater Control Over Blue Helmets," *Foreign Policy*, October 2, 2016, available at <http://foreignpolicy.com/2016/10/02/china-eyes-ending-western-grip-on-top-u-n-jobs-with-greater-control-over-blue-helmets/>.

147 Mo Yinglong and Wan Chusheng, "PLA Is to Send a Peacekeeping Medical Team to Liberia," *PLA Daily*, November 18, 2003, available at <http://english.chinamil.com.cn/english/pladaily/2003/11/18/20031118001014_militarynews.html>; Guo Renjie, "PLA Sends First Medical Team to Fight Against Ebola in Sierra Leone," *China Military Online*, September 17, 2014, available at <http://eng.chinamil.com.cn/news-channels/china-military-news/2014-09/17/content_6142314.htm>; Mengjie, "Chinese Medical Team Stays in Liberia to Fight Ebola," Xinhua, August 2, 2014, available at <http://news.Xinhuanet.com/english/china/2014-08/02/c_133526735.htm>. Several other articles were used to provide a list of every peacekeeping medical detachments since 2004.

148 Xiang Bo, "Nine Chinese Aircraft Finish Ebola Rescue Task," Xinhua, November 19, 2014, available at <http://news.xinhuanet.com/english/china/2014-11/19/c_133801063.htm>.

149 Erickson and Strange.

150 Zhang Zhihao, "Naval Escort Fleet Returns After Successful Gulf of Aden Mission," *China Daily*, November 3, 2016, available at <www.chinadaily.com.cn/china/2016-11/03/content_27263994.htm>.

151 "Chinese Naval Escort Taskforces Complete Mission Handover," *China Military Online*, January 3, 2017, available at <http://eng.mod.gov.cn/DefenseNews/2017-01/03/content_4769046.htm>; Zhu Ke, "China Naval Special Forces 'Dragon Commando': 300 Days of Gulf of Aden Escorts [中国海军特种部队蛟龙突击队：亚丁湾护航300天]," *China.com*, February 5, 2010, available at <www.china.com.cn/military/txt/2010-02/05/content_19373527_2.htm>; PLA special forces are organized into regiment-level *dadui* (大队) and are separate from the PLAN's Marine Corps.

152 For an excellent description of the *Peace Ark*'s expanding role in the PLAN's overseas presence, see Peter W. Mackenzie, "Red Crosses, Blue Water: Hospital Ships and China's Expanding Naval Presence," Center for Naval Analyses, September 2011. See also Kyle Mizokami, "Peace Ark: Onboard China's Hospital Ship," *USNI News*, July 23, 2014, available at <http://news.usni.org/2014/07/23/peace-ark-onboard-chinas-hospital-ship>; Fang Lihua and Ju Zhenhua, "Spreading Friendship and Compassion to 16 Nations and Tempering Capabilities While Journeying Across the Worlds' Oceans—Peace Ark: The Impressive Calling Card for a Responsible Nation [倾情播撒友谊爱播十六国眠断能力航迹遍及工三洋—和平方舟：负责任大国形象的亮丽名片]," *Renmin Haijun*, November 11, 2013.

153 Kamlesh Kumar Agnihotri, "China's 'Peace Ark': The Navy and Band-aid Diplomacy," IPCS Article 4026, July 9, 2013, available at <www.ipcs.org/article/military/chinas-peace-ark-the-navy-and-band-aid-diplomacy-4026.html>; Mizokami; Zhang Tao, "Australian Military Doctors Join Chinese Ship," *China Military Online*, September 10, 2014, available at <http://eng.chinamil.com.cn/news-channels/china-military-news/2014-09/10/content_6131160.htm>.

154 Zhang Tao, ed., "Chinese Hospital Ship Peace Ark Set Out for Harmonious Mission–2015," *China Military Online*, September 25, 2015, available at <http://english.chinamil.com.cn/news-channels/china-military-news/2015-09/25/content_6699367.htm>.

155 Li Xiao and Hu Quanfu, "Chinese Navy Escort Transport of Syria's Chemistry Weapons," *China Armed Forces* 1, no. 25 (2014), 82–87; Kong Defang and Yan Meng, eds., "Chinese Navy to Escort Transportation of Syria's Chemical Weapons," *People's Daily*, January 2, 2014, available at <http://eng-

lish.people.com.cn/90786/8501590.html>.

[156] Qiang Lijing, "Timeline: China's Military in the Search for MH370," *China Armed Forces* 2, no. 26 (2014), 12–17; Meng Jinyu, "Aerial Search for MH370 [空中搜寻MH370]," *China Air Force*, April 2014, 36–38; Yao Jianing, "Ten Breakthroughs of China's Military Diplomacy in 2014 (1)."

[157] Yang Lina and Chang Xuemei, eds., "Xi Jinping: Start a New Phase of Military Diplomacy [习近平：进一步开创军事外交新局面]," Xinhua, January 29, 2015, available at <http://cpc.people.com.cn/n/2015/0129/c64094-26474947.html>.

[158] All these military diplomatic interactions are recorded in the dataset, which is available for download on the NDU Press Web site.

[159] Authors' interview with PLA flag officer, 2014.

[160] The Europe region does not include Russia, which was counted as a separate region in order to better examine its relative importance. A full accounting of PLA military diplomatic activity by country and region is included in the appendix.

[161] The authors' interactions with the Japanese and South Korean militaries indicate that the reduction in interactions was due to decisions made by the Chinese side.

[162] In addition to the 10 Association of South East Asian Nations countries, we include Australia, New Zealand, and other countries in Oceania in the Southeast Asia subregion.

[163] The differentials were calculated as the difference between meetings hosted in China and meetings held abroad.

[164] Zhang Wei, "On Study of the Theory of Chinese Military Diplomacy [关于中国军事外交的理论探讨]," *China Military Science* 3 [中国军事科学] (2004), 34; Chen Zhiyong, 35–36, 39.

[165] For a comprehensive listing and taxonomy of Chinese strategic partnerships and relationships, see Peter Wood and Matt G. Brazil, "China's Foreign Relations: Levels of Commitment," available at <https://www.p-wood.co/2016/09/18/chinas-foreign-relations/>.

[166] Scott L. Kastner and Phillip C. Saunders, "Exploring China's Strategic Partnerships: Characteristics, Motivations, and Consequences," paper presented at the International Studies Association, March 26, 2014, 2; Su Hao, "The 'Partnership' Frame in China's Foreign Affairs [中国外交的’伙伴关系’框架]," *World Knowledge* [世界知识] 5 (2000).

[167] Kastner and Saunders, 4–6.

[168] Feng Zhongping and Huang Jing, "China's Strategic Partnership Diplomacy: Engaging with a Changing World," European Strategic Partnerships Observatory, Working Paper 8, June 2014, available at <http://papers.ssrn.com/sol3/papers.cfm?abstract_id=2459948>.

[169] Joel Wuthnow, *Posing Problems Without an Alliance: China-Iran Relations after the Nuclear Deal*, INSS Strategic Forum 290 (Washington, DC: NDU Press, February 2016), 1.

[170] Franz Stefan-Gady, "China and Russia to Hold First Computer-Enabled Missile Defense Exercise in May," *The Diplomat*, May 2, 2016, available at <http://thediplomat.com/2016/05/china-and-russia-to-hold-first-computer-enabled-missile-defense-exercise-in-may/>.

[171] Chu Yongzheng, 117.

[172] See Dean Cheng, *Cyber Dragon: Inside China's Information Warfare and Cyber Operations* (Denver, CO: Praeger, 2017).

[173] Wan Fayang.

[174] Authors' experience, among others.

[175] "U.S., Chinese Navies Practice Search and Rescue, CUES," USS *Benfold* Public Affairs, Office of the Commander, United States Pacific Fleet, August 15, 2016, available at <http://www.cpf.navy.mil/news.aspx/130061>.

[176] Chu Yongzheng, 137–141.

[177] Nuclear Threat Initiative, "Proposed Prevention of an Arms Race in Space (Paros) Treaty," March 25, 2015, available at <www.nti.org/learn/treaties-and-regimes/proposed-prevention-arms-race-space-paros-treaty/>. The full draft is available at <http://i.cfr.org/content/publications/attachments/PPWT.pdf>.

About the Authors

Mr. Kenneth Allen is the Research Director of the China Aerospace Studies Institute at the U.S. Air Force. For the past 25 years, his primary focus has been on the Chinese military's organizational structure, personnel, education, training, and foreign relations, with particular emphasis on the People's Liberation Army (PLA) Air Force. He previously worked for the U.S.-Taiwan Business Council, Henry L. Stimson Center, Litton TASC, Center for Naval Analysis, Defense Group, Inc., and Long Term Strategy Group. During his 21 years in the U.S. Air Force (1971–1992), he served as an enlisted Chinese and Russian linguist and intelligence officer with tours in Taiwan, Germany, Japan, PACAF Headquarters, China, and Washington, DC (Instructor in the Defense Intelligence Agency [DIA] Joint Military Attaché School). From 1987–1989, he served as the Assistant Air Attaché in the U.S. Embassy in Beijing, where he received the individual Exceptional Collector of the Year Award for 1988 and the Unit Exceptional Collector of the Year Award for 1989 (Tiananmen). He was inducted into DIA's Defense Attaché Hall of Fame in 1997. He has BAs from the University of California at Davis and University of Maryland, and an MA from Boston University. He has written multiple books, monographs, book chapters, journal articles, and online articles on the PLA.

Dr. Phillip C. Saunders is Director of the Center for the Study of Chinese Military Affairs (CSCMA) and a Distinguished Research Fellow, Institute for National Strategic Studies, at the National Defense University. Dr. Saunders previously worked at the Monterey Institute of International Studies, where he was Director of the East Asia Nonproliferation Program from 1999–2003, and served as an officer in the U.S. Air Force from 1989–1994. Dr. Saunders is co-author, with David Gompert, of *The Paradox of Power: Sino-American Strategic Restraint in an Era of Vulnerability* (NDU Press, 2011) and co-editor of five books on Chinese military and security issues. Dr. Saunders attended Harvard College and received his MPA and Ph.D. in International Relations from the Woodrow Wilson School at Princeton University.

Mr. John Chen is a Research Associate at Defense Group, Inc., where he conducts China-related research and analysis on foreign policy, national security, and science and technology issues using Chinese-language sources. Previously, he was a research intern in CSCMA and received an AB from Dartmouth College and an MA from Georgetown University.

www.ingramcontent.com/pod-product-compliance
Lightning Source LLC
Chambersburg PA
CBHW080725260726
48660CB00010B/3705